T0064833

INGRID & PELLE HOLMBERG

# WILD MUSHROOM COOKBOOK

## SOUPS, STIR-FRIES, AND FULL COURSES FROM THE FOREST TO THE FRYING PAN

PHOTOGRAPHY BY SUSANNE HALLMANN
TRANSLATED BY ELLEN HEDSTRÖM

SKYHORSE PUBLISHING

*Thank you, Dieter Endom and Jens Linder*
*for sharing your wealth of culinary knowledge with us.*
*Thanks also to all the mushroom experts, neighbors,*
*relatives, and friends who have contributed to this book.*

Copyright © 2012 by Ingrid and Pelle Holmberg and Norstedts, Stockholm
English translation © 2014 by Skyhorse Publishing
Design by Typerna/Seth Kapadia
Photography by Susanne Hallmann
First published by Norstedts, Sweden in 2012 as *Svampkokboken* by Ingrid and Pelle Holmberg.
Published by agreement with Norstedts Agency.

Skyhorse Publishing books may be purchased in bulk at special discounts for sales promotion, corporate gifts, fund-raising, or educational purposes. Special editions can also be created to specifications. For details, contact the Special Sales Department, Skyhorse Publishing, 307 West 36th Street, 11th Floor, New York, NY 10018 or info@skyhorsepublishing.com

Skyhorse® and Skyhorse Publishing® are registered trademarks of Skyhorse Publishing, Inc.®, a Delaware corporation.

www.skyhorsepublishing.com

10 9 8 7 6 5 4 3 2

Library of Congress Cataloging-in-Publication Data is available on file.

ISBN: 978-1-62914-420-7
Ebook ISBN: 978-1-63220-190-4

Cover design by Danielle Ceccolini

Printed in China

# CONTENTS

# FOREWORD

Ten years ago we published the original *Wild Mushroom Cookbook* in Swedish together with the chef Dieter Endom. Dieter was the first chef to train as a mushroom expert, and it was fun as well educational to work with him. Dieter also contributed some of his best recipes to this book with some, so we would like to extend a big thank you to him!

We hope our new mushroom cookbook will inspire you to experiment more when you cook with mushrooms, as there is a lot more you can do than just frying them or preparing them in creamy sauces.

For almost forty years, we have together picked and prepared mushrooms of every variety. Pelle is a biologist and the author of roughly twenty books on nature. He has met tens of thousands of mushroom enthusiasts during his career and has even been involved in educating some of Sweden's mushroom experts, several of whom have contributed to this book.

Ingrid has participated in many excursions and exhibitions. Sometimes, we give tasting sessions where we serve mushroom soup or something similar, and many people ask us for recipes and tips on how to prepare the mushrooms they've picked.

In our home, Pelle is the resident mushroom picker and over the years he has often set off before anyone else has woken up and returned just in time for breakfast with a few quarts of wild strawberries, gallons of blueberries, or multiple baskets filled with mushrooms.

Thankfully, Ingrid loves cooking and happily prepares most of what Pelle brings home. Some of our favorite memories have come from working together to prepare the harvest from nature's pantry, both from the woods and our garden.

Mushrooms and berries have always been a welcome addition when we cook—especially when our four children were small and money was tight. Berries and mushrooms added something extra to our everyday lives and helped us stretch the household budget. Now our children are grown, we are delighted to see that they, as well as their friends, enjoy picking mushrooms and berries. Every fall we make an improvised mushroom excursion with the kids and their families, friends, and their friends' parents.

We hope you will be inspired by our book to add some flavor to your own cooking with these wonderful mushrooms!

INGRID *and* PELLE HOLMBERG

# PICKING AND CARING FOR YOUR MUSHROOMS

Surely not everyone picks as many mushrooms as we do. We don't merely have one basket filled with mushrooms—one time Pelle came home with five banana boxes stuffed with Porcini! Thankfully the majority of the cleaning was done on site.

The best weather to pick mushrooms is when it's overcast but not raining. On sunny days, it can be hard to spot the mushrooms; in rainy weather, the mushrooms get wet and may fall apart easily.

When picking mushrooms, you should have a decent and airy basket, a knife, and a brush. You can buy special mushroom knives with a brush on the handle, but sometimes this brush can be too soft; if you have one of these, cut off the ends of the bristles.

Never put picked mushrooms in a plastic bag, as the bag quickly gets warm and humid, which means that the mushrooms can start to degrade and spoil. In an emergency, you can use a paper bag.

Only pick mushrooms that you can identify with certainty. If you want to learn more, take a course. At the very least, buy a good, up-to-date mushroom book that is designed for edible mushrooms in your local environment. There are books that may be written in your language but are about a different environment than your own. Many mushrooms have also been reclassified in the past few years. In older books, you may find that mushrooms that are no longer considered safe are classified as edible and even tasty. If you find different information in different books, always trust the information in the latest edition.

## Picking and removing dirt

When it comes to cleaning the mushrooms, doing the major work on site will make it so much easier to clean them when you get home. Remember never to pick more than you are able to clean and care for, preferably on the same day as they are picked.

Pick up the whole mushroom, including the base of the stipe so that you are able to see all the important characteristics needed to identify the mushroom. Smell the mushroom and make sure it smells the way it ought to. Once you are sure of the mushroom's identity, cut off the portion of the base of the stipe that is covered in dirt. If the mushroom is large, cut it in half to see if it has been attacked by maggots. Throw away any mushroom that is too infested. If it is not too badly infested, remove only those parts that have been affected. Any tubes that are attached can be left. Remove any pine needles and dirt with a brush before placing the mushroom in a basket.

If you have found a mushroom that you need to take home in order to identify it further, place it in a separate part of the basket. It is always worth cutting up a milk carton or bringing a plastic tub to place these mushrooms in to avoid mixing them in with the edible mushrooms.

Upon your return, you will have a basket filled with clean, maggot-free mushrooms, which will be quite helpful once you sit down to start the finer cleaning.

### Cleaning

Place the mushrooms on a table and sort them into piles by mushroom type. Start with cleaning the Russulas and Boletales, which are the most sensitive. Chanterelles, Trumpet Chanterelles, Black Trumpets, and Yellow Foot can survive for several days if they are placed in the fridge and are well ventilated.

Remove the slimy skin off the caps of mushrooms such as the Slippery Jack and the Slimy Spike Cap. Needles and debris attached to the caps can be removed with the rough side of a damp kitchen sponge or a scouring pad. Mushrooms that need to be precooked or blanched can be rinsed if they are dirty. Ideally,

mushrooms that are going to be dried should not be rinsed, as they need to be as dry as possible. Remove the spongy pore surface if you haven't already done so in the woods. Remove any parts infested by maggots; if there are only a few small maggot holes, the mushroom is fine to use.

Consider your plans for the mushrooms. Do you want to freeze them? Dry them? Do you want them in small or large pieces? Are there any Milk Caps that need to be concentrated? mushrooms that are to be precooked, which means blanched in their own juices, should be chopped straight into a pan. Mushrooms to be dried should be cut or sliced straight onto a mushroom dryer, and the machine switched on. Mushrooms that have been cleaned and chopped can be placed in various containers, depending on what you plan to do with them.

If you have a poor harvest with only a few mushrooms, your best bet is to cook them all together and enjoy eating them fresh.

Please note that both the person picking the mushrooms and the person cleaning them at home need to be certain of the identity of the mushrooms.

### Storing

The most common way to store mushrooms is to freeze or dry them. Pickling and preserving in jars were methods used before freezers were invented.

## Freezing

Mushrooms can be frozen fresh but take up a lot of space. Clean the mushrooms and then either leave them whole or divide them into pieces. Place into bags or containers and freeze, marking them with the date and contents.

Most people cook the mushrooms before freezing them. To do this, place the clean, chopped mushrooms in a pan to slowly simmer in their own juices. Don't let the liquid boil away completely, and if the mushrooms get too dry you can add some water. The liquid protects the mushrooms so that they don't get "freezer burn" when frozen. Allow the mushrooms to cool and place them in containers or freezer bags. It can be hard to see the contents when they are frozen, so always write the contents and date on the bag.

Make sure the freezer is cold enough and never warmer than 0°F (–18°C). Some freezers have a button for preserving food, and if you have large quantities to freeze you can make use of this.

If you have a lot of mushrooms that you wish to freeze, you can always blanche the mushrooms first. Place cleaned and chopped mushrooms in a pan of enough boiling water to barely cover the mushrooms. Bring to a boil again and cook for about a minute. Remove the mushrooms but keep the water to use for the next batch. Rinse the mushrooms in cold water and place in bags or containers. When you have finished cooking all the mushrooms, you can pour a small amount of the blanched water into the bags or containers to cover the mushrooms. Write the contents and date on the packaging.

There are several advantages to blanching: it's quick, it gives the mushrooms a nice consistency, and Boletales will be less slimy. Blanched mushrooms are quicker to fry and do not soak up as much fat as fresh or blanched mushrooms.

When it comes to Russulas, however, it is usually better to precook (or dry) than to blanche. The skin on the cap will add color to the precooked mushrooms and the red Crab Brittlegills take on a lovely pink hue—an effect that disappears when blanched.

What about the taste? Doesn't this disappear when blanched? We find the mushrooms taste the same after blanching, and we think it is so effective that we often blanch fresh mushrooms, and even cultivated Button mushrooms, before we cook them. We have even cooked mushrooms in broth.

The liquid that remains can be used as broth, but if you have been cooking Boletales in the water it can turn slimy and should be discarded.

NOTE: The mushrooms need to cool completely before being placed in the freezer.

## Drying

Dried mushrooms are very useful, and Boletales are especially suited to this, as drying removes their sliminess—the Velvet Bolete in particular tastes a lot nicer dried than fresh. Remember that dried mushrooms often have a stronger taste

than fresh mushrooms do, so it's better to use too little than too much when cooking with them.

The chewy stipe on the Parasol mushroom is great to dry and turn into mushroom flour. Divide the stipes along the fibers and allow them to dry—they usually dry very quickly at room temperature.

Dried mushrooms don't take up a lot of space, and if you use only what you need, they will last a long time. Nils and Astrid Suber served thirty-year-old dried Parasol mushrooms to Pelle, and he says they tasted excellent. However, we do not recommend keeping dried mushrooms for this long, and it's best if you try to empty the pantry and freezer of mushrooms in time for the next mushroom season.

Thin mushrooms, such as the Trumpet Chanterelle (*Craterellus tubaeformis*), Yellow Foot (*Craterellus lutescens*), or Black Trumpet, can be dried at room temperature. Pull the mushrooms apart, as insects and debris can often be found in the funnel.

Place them on a sheet or a thin fabric on top of a newspaper or a piece of corrugated cardboard and place in a well-ventilated area. Alternatively, place them in baskets that allow air to circulate. Turn the mushrooms from time to time; they should be bone dry after three days at the latest.

Thicker mushrooms need a source of heat to dry, and a drying machine is normally the best option and can even be used to dry fruits, berries, and herbs. There are several varieties on the market.

You can also make your own dryer. The mushrooms need to be placed so they are spaced out, preferably in a drying box. An insect screen can be used and should be placed over a fan in a drying cupboard, or in another dry and well-ventilated location. Check regularly that the mushrooms remain fresh. They should be dry within a maximum of three days.

You can also use an oven to dry mushrooms, but the temperature should not exceed 125°F (50°C) as this will make them black and bitter.

The mushrooms should be chopped into pieces of equal size; the thinner they are, the faster they dry. If you are using a drying machine, read the instructions and remember: never dry mushrooms at a temperature above 125°F (50°C)!

Store in glass jars with lids and label them with the date and contents, especially if you are storing a large quantity of mushrooms.

*Salting*

In Finland, Russia, and other Eastern European countries, it is common to salt mushrooms, and all types of mushrooms can be salted.

Clean and slice the mushrooms and cook them in their own juices. Layer mushrooms and salt in a glass jar or pot, using about ⅔ cup (200 ml) coarse salt for around every quart (1 liter) of mushrooms that have been blanched or concentrated (see below regarding the Northern Milk Cap (*Lactarius trivialis*) and the Rufous Milk Cap. Place a plate on top so that the mushroom is submerged in the salty brine that is produced.

If you are planning on salting the Northern Milk Cap or Rufous Milk Cap, they must be blanched first. Clean the mushrooms and cut into pieces; small Milk Caps can be left whole. Place the mushrooms in a saucepan with very cold water and boil for 10–20 minutes. Discard the water and rinse the mushrooms. Then layer the mushrooms and salt as described above.

Store the salted mushrooms in a cool place; when they are ready to be used, they need to be soaked for 8–10 hours in plenty of cold water.

## Preserving

When heated, the microorganisms in the mushrooms are destroyed. The air expands and dissipates under the rubber seal; when the jar cools, the air in the jar contracts; the lid is so firmly attached that no outside air can get in.

Clean and slice the mushrooms. Small mushrooms can be left whole. Place the mushrooms in a saucepan and add ½ tsp salt for each quart (liter) of mushrooms. Boil the mushrooms, covered, in their own juices for 10 minutes.

Fill clean preserving jars, leaving a ¾ inch (2 cm) space at the top. Boil the rubber seal for a minute or so in water before attaching it to the lid. Close the jars and place a towel or something similar in the bottom of a pot and place the jar on top. Fill the pot with water until it is two-thirds of the way full, and boil over a low heat for 1¼ hours. Allow the jars to cool in the pot, then remove them and place on a towel while they cool completely. Store the jars in a cool, dark place.

# COOKING MUSHROOMS

Mushrooms can be hard to digest and need to be cooked properly for at least 10–20 minutes, if not more. A creamy sauce or soup tastes better the longer you leave it to simmer. At the chemistry center (Kemicentrum) in Lund, Sweden, studies by Börje Wickberg and his colleagues have shown that various toxins found in mushrooms, or that appear when the mushroom is damaged, can be poisonous if the mushroom is consumed raw. If the mushroom is heated, these substances are rendered safe, which means it's better for our health to eat cooked mushrooms.

## Fresh mushrooms

Place the sliced or whole mushrooms in a frying pan or saucepan and slowly let them cook in their own juices until the liquid is completely evaporated. Add butter or oil. For creamy sauces and soups, the mushrooms only need to be fried a few minutes.

If the mushrooms are to be served fried, fry them until golden brown.

You can also heat the fat first and then fry the mushrooms in it. This works best with mushrooms that are drier; these need to be thinly sliced. Don't add too much at a time, as they will boil rather than fry. Let any liquid completely evaporate.

Boletales can easily turn slimy when precooked, so it's better to quickly blanche them. Place the mushrooms in boiling water—just enough to cover them—and boil rapidly. Remove the liquid and fry. This also works well with Chanterelles, Trumpet Chanterelles, Sheep Polypores, Wood Hedgehogs, and Button mushrooms.

## Frozen mushrooms

Thaw frozen mushrooms and remove the liquid using a colander, but save the liquid. Fry some butter or oil in a saucepan or frying pan and prepare as above. The liquid can be used for soup, or sauces, or for adding a little at a time to the pan while frying.

## Dried mushrooms

Dried mushrooms should be placed in cold, lukewarm, or hot water. The thinner the pieces, the quicker it goes—just test the mushroom to see if it is soft. Remove the water and keep it to use when preparing the dish.

Dried Black Trumpet has a strong taste, so don't use too much. In this case, remove the water, as it will turn black and give the dish a dirty gray color.

Fry the soaked mushrooms in fat and add a little of the liquid if it looks too dry.

You can also crumble dried mushroom straight into soups, sauces, or risotto. Don't forget it needs to cook for at least 10 minutes.

Dried mushrooms can be ground into mushroom flour, which can then be used to flavor dishes.

### Preserved mushrooms

Preserved mushrooms are prepared in the same way as frozen mushrooms. The liquid can also be retained and reused.

### Salted mushrooms

Salted mushrooms have to be soaked for 8–10 hours before they can be used; see page 11.

### Store-bought mushrooms

If you are a mushroom fan, you often want fresh mushrooms, even when there are none to be picked. Well-stocked grocery stores often have a variety of mushrooms, such as Button mushrooms, Portobellos, Oyster mushrooms, and Shiitakes.

We often mix store-bought mushrooms with those we have picked ourselves. Mixing wild mushrooms with store-bought ones can create new flavors.

The Oyster mushroom is mild in flavor and pairs well with Chanterelles. If you only have a few Chanterelles, you can buy some Oyster mushrooms to pad them out.

Don't hesitate to use store-bought mushrooms in the recipes found in this book. We often recommend different mushrooms that can be substituted for those in the recipe.

### Conversion chart

It is hard to say how much a quart or liter of mushrooms really is, as it depends on the size of the pieces and how wet or dry the mushrooms are. It's the same with dried mushrooms; it depends on the size of the pieces and how tightly packed they are. We have created a chart (below) that shows roughly how much cooked and dried mushrooms you get from fresh ones. We hope this makes it easy for you to adapt the recipes to the mushrooms you want to use. 1 quart (1 liter) of fresh mushrooms yields about 1¼ cups (300 ml) of cooked, or just under ½–1¼ cups (100–300 ml) dried mushrooms.

Frozen, precooked mushrooms are calculated in the same way as precooked mushrooms in this table.

| FRESH MUSHROOMS | PRECOOKED MUSHROOMS | DRIED MUSHROOMS | MUSHROOM FLOUR |
|---|---|---|---|
| 1 quart (1 liter)........... | 1¼ cups (300 ml)........... | ½–1¼ cups (100–300 ml).... | ½ cup (100 ml) |
| 7–10½ oz (200–300 g)... | 7–10½ oz (200–300 g)...... | ¾–1 oz (20–30 g)........... | ¾–1 oz (20–30 g) |

# MUSHROOM FLOUR

*Mushroom flour is a great kitchen staple. You can add it to soups and sauces to give them a mushroom flavor, and, if you have lots of fresh but mild-tasting mushrooms, you can sprinkle them with mushroom flour to increase the taste.*

- dried mushrooms, any variety

Learn how to dry mushrooms on page 9. When the mushrooms are bone dry, you can put them through a food processor, using the chopping blade, until they turn to flour. Store the flour in a glass jar with a lid; it's a good idea to write on the jar what type of mushroom was used.

You can make flour from all types of mushrooms. Boletales are great when dried, as all the sliminess disappears. The Velvet Bolete also tastes a lot better dried than fresh. Mushroom flour from Weeping Milk Cap makes a great spice for seafood dishes, and I often dry the stipe of Parasol mushrooms, which is woody and chewy to prepare but makes great mushroom flour. If you pull the stipes apart along the fibers and let them air out in a basket or something similar, they will dry quickly.

The flour can be used to bread ingredients, either on its own or mixed with breadcrumbs or wheat flour. ¼ cup (100 ml/20–30 g) of mushroom flour is equivalent to at least a quart (1 liter) of fresh mushrooms, so it's better to use sparingly than to use too much when adding flavor, as dried mushrooms can taste very strong.

# MUSHROOM STOCK

*Inger Ingmanson has written several books on the topic of foraging for food, from herbs to wild meat. Below is her recipe for mushroom stock. It's important to use dried mushrooms, as otherwise the stock will become slimy. Feel free to dry some woody stipes to use when making the stock.*

- 1¼ cup (500 ml) dried mushrooms (1¾ oz/50 g)
- 1 piece of fresh ginger, peeled
- 4 inches (10 cm) of leek
- 2 tsp soy sauce
- 2 tsp fat
- a few peppercorns
- 1 quart (1 liter) water or chicken stock

Place all the ingredients in a pot and pour in the water. Cover and place in the oven for 2 hours at a temperature of 300°F (150°C). Strain the stock and season to taste. The stock can be used as a consommé with a bit of chervil or parsley. You can also whip together some cream and an egg yolk in a bowl and pour the hot stock over top.

Freeze the stock in an ice cube tray and use to flavor dishes.

The stock can also be preserved in glass jars—make sure you use jars with rubber sealing rings. The jars need to be completely clean. Boil the rubber rings for a few minutes and fill the jars, leaving a ¾ inch (2 cm) gap at the top. Put the rubber seal on the lid and close the jar. Place the jar on a folded towel that has been placed into a large pan and add just enough water to cover the jar. Bring to a boil and then simmer over low heat for an hour. Then, allow the jars to cool in the water. Remove and allow to cool completely under a towel. Store in a cool, dark location.

Any remaining mushrooms will have retained some flavor and can be used (unless just the woody stipes are leftover). Fry together with some bacon or bacon fat.

# ST. GEORGE'S MUSHROOM SOUP WITH NETTLES AND GROUND ELDER

*Every time we have this soup, we wonder why we don't make it more often. Soups are easy to prepare and can be made from almost anything, and, if you add some mushrooms, they become even better.*

4 PORTIONS

- ½ quart (½ liter) fresh St. George's mushrooms
- approx. 1 quart (1 liter) nettles
- 1½ cups (200 ml) chopped ground elder
- 1 small onion, finely chopped
- butter or oil
- 1 quart (1 liter) water
- 2 tbsp wheat flour, optional
- 1–2 bouillon cubes, chicken or vegetable
- 1–2 tbsp cream, optional
- chervil
- 2 tbsp chopped ramsons, shallot, or chives
- salt and pepper

Finely slice the St. George's mushrooms. These have quite a specific taste that can be diluted by boiling them first. Place the mushrooms in plenty of cold water and bring to a boil. Boil for 5 minutes and then discard the water.

Clean the nettles and place in boiling water. Boil for a few minutes and then drain the water. Finely chop the nettles. Fry onions, mushrooms, and ground elder in a little butter or oil over low heat until the onion is translucent. Boil some water. If you want to thicken the soup, you can slowly add flour and dilute with hot liquid while stirring. If not, just add the hot liquid to the onion mixture. Crumble the bouillon cubes into the mixture and bring to a boil. Cook for about 10 minutes.

Add the nettles and cook for another 5 minutes. You can add cream at this stage if you like. Season to taste with salt, pepper, and chervil, and sprinkle some ramsons, shallot, or chives on top.

You can make this soup with spinach and other mushroom varieties, but it's ideal to use seasonal ingredients. This particular variant a true spring soup.

# PELLE'S MUSHROOM SOUP

*We've made Pelle's mushroom soup many a time over the years. It's great to serve when guests are visiting, and with some nice bread, cheeses, a fancy table setting, and a delicious dessert, you can make this the base of a proper gourmet meal.*

4 PORTIONS

- 1½ quart (1½ liters) fresh, mixed mushrooms or the equivalent amount frozen or dried (1 lb/450 g)
- 1 yellow onion, chopped
- 1 small carrot, chopped
- celeriac (same amount as the carrot, chopped), optional
- 2 tbsp butter
- 1 quart (1 liter) water
- 2 bouillon cubes, chicken or vegetable
- 2 tbsp wheat flour or 4 tbsp light cornstarch
- ¼ cup (50 ml) crème fraîche or sour cream
- parsley
- salt and pepper

Chop the mushrooms and fry with the onion, carrots, and celeriac (optional) in the butter until most of the liquid is absorbed. If you are using dried mushrooms, they will need to be soaked first. In that case, you can fry the onion, carrots, and celeriac (optional) while you are waiting, and then add the soaked mushrooms once they are ready. Add some water if it is too dry.

Add the water and crumble the stock cubes into the mixture. Boil for at least 10 minutes.

Mix the flour or corn starch with a little water and add to the soup while stirring. Cook for 5 minutes. The cornstarch can be added directly into the soup. Finally, add the crème fraîche and bring to a boil. Season to taste with salt and pepper and sprinkle some chopped parsley on top.

This is a simple, everyday soup, and we think it works best with dried mushrooms. The soup can vary in taste depending on which mushrooms are used. If you mainly use mild-flavored mushrooms, you can add more flavor by using mushroom flour. I sometimes use a dash of lime or lemon juice, too. Root vegetables work well together with mushrooms, and sometimes I might use a parsnip. If you are having a party, you can substitute some of the water for white wine or add a dash of cognac or sherry; you can also increase the amount of crème fraîche used to give it that gourmet feel. Try blending the soup until completely smooth and add a few pieces of fried mushrooms just before serving.

# FISH SOUP, WITH OR WITHOUT FISH

*The Crab Brittlegill and Weeping Milk Cap both taste of shellfish. Try them with other, milder mushrooms to make the flavor less intense but just as tasty. The Weeping Milk Cap is not so common, so if you do stumble upon some, feel free to dry any extras to use as flavoring. You don't need a large amount to get this mushroom's unique taste.*

- 2–6 cups (½–1½ liters) fresh Crab Brittlegill and Weeping Milk Caps
- 1 tbsp canola oil
- 1 carrot, roughly grated
- 1 leek, sliced
- 1–2 stalks of celery, sliced
- 1 quart (1 liter) of fish stock, ideally made from a bouillon cube or homemade (see below)
- 1 tbsp lime or lemon juice
- 3 tbsp light cornstarch
- 11 oz (300 g) fillet of fish, chopped into smaller chunks (optional)
- ½ cup (100 ml) peas (optional)
- dill
- salt and pepper

If you plan to skip the fresh fish, use more mushrooms, and vice versa. Chop the Crab Brittlegills into pieces; the Weeping Milk Caps can be grated. Fry the mushrooms in some of the oil over low heat for 10–15 minutes. Add water if it gets too dry. Fry the carrot and leek in a saucepan using the rest of the oil.

Add the fried mushrooms and celery. Pour in the stock and bring to a boil. Thicken the soup when the vegetables are almost cooked through and return to boiling. Add the fish and then simmer until cooked through. If you like, you can add some peas at this stage. Add salt and pepper to taste and sprinkle some chopped dill on top.

*Stock:* If you buy fresh fish, ask to have it filleted and ask to keep the head and carcass, removing the gills. Place the head and carcass (approx. 1 lb–1⅔ lb/500–750 g) in a saucepan, add a quart of water (1 liter) and bring to a boil, skimming off the fat. Add 2 tsp salt, 5 white peppercorns, the green part of the leek that you will be using in your soup, 1 small carrot, 1 celery stalk, or a few leaves of lovage, and some dill stalks. Cook over low heat for at least 20 minutes. If you plan to use dried Weeping Milk Cap, you can add it to the stock. When you strain the stock, you can pick out the mushroom pieces and cut them into thin slices, which can then be added to the soup.

# TRUMPET CHANTERELLE SOUP WITH GORGONZOLA

*Per-Axel Karlsson is the mushroom expert chairman, and he is fanatical about food. His Trumpet Chanterelle Soup with Gorgonzola has been a favorite for many years, and not just with mushroom experts!*

4 PORTIONS

- 2 quarts (2 liters) fresh Trumpet Chanterelles
- 2–3 tbsp butter
- 1 yellow onion, chopped
- 2 tbsp wheat flour
- 2 tsp mushroom flour, optional (see p. 17)
- 1 quart (1 liter) chicken or mushroom stock made from a bouillon cube
- 1 tsp capers
- 1¾ oz (50 g) gorgonzola
- 2 tbsp crème fraîche or sour cream
- ½ lemon, juice
- cayenne pepper
- ¼ cup (50 ml) port wine
- approx. 1¾ oz (50 g) arugula
- fresh basil
- salt

Place the Trumpet Chanterelles in a pot and precook them to remove all the liquid. Remove a quarter of the mushrooms and fry over low heat until they are slightly crunchy. Set aside to be used when serving.

Add the butter and onion to the pot and fry until the onion is translucent. Sprinkle some wheat flour and, if you like, some mushroom flour on top. Add the warm stock and bring to a boil, stirring continuously. Leave to simmer for 10 minutes.

Mix the soup with the capers, gorgonzola, and crème fraîche, and bring to a boil, seasoning with lemon juice, cayenne pepper, wine, and salt.

Shred the arugula and place in the soup, simmering for a few minutes. Pour the soup into warm bowls and garnish with the fried mushrooms and some basil.

# TINA'S BEST TRUMPET CHANTERELLE SOUP

Tina is a former colleague who loves to walk in the woods to pick mushrooms or bird watch. This is her favorite soup, which she originally found on a supermarket recipe card. Chef Sander Johansson created the dish.

**4 PORTIONS**

- 1 quart (1 liter) fresh Trumpet Chanterelles or 1 oz (30 g) dried
- 1 yellow onion, finely chopped
- 2 tbsp butter
- 2 tsp tomato puree
- 3 tbsp wheat flour
- 1 quart (1 liter) water
- 2 mushroom or vegetable bouillon cubes
- ¾ cup (200 ml) crème fraîche or sour cream
- 2 tbsp dry sherry
- 1 pinch salt
- 1 pinch cayenne pepper
- 1 pinch pepper

*To serve:*
- crème fraîche or sour cream
- red onion, finely chopped
- fresh thyme

Soak the dried mushrooms and discard the water. Roughly chop the mushrooms and fry them and the onion in butter until the liquid is absorbed. Mix in the tomato puree and flour, add the water, and crumble the bouillon cubes into the mixture. Bring to a boil and add the crème fraîche and sherry. Cook for about 10–15 minutes, then season to taste.

Serve with crème fraîche, finely chopped red onion, and fresh thyme.

You can use parsley instead of thyme, and you can also swap the Trumpet Chanterelles for Black Trumpets, False Saffron Milk Caps, or a combination of mixed mushrooms.

# MAGGAN'S FALSE SAFFRON MILK CAP SOUP

*My sister-in-law Margareta has given me many great recipes. She had a lot of False Saffron Milk Caps in her freezer that she wanted to use and found a recipe that she adapted to suit her tastes. My brother-in-law, Lasse, was really waxing poetic over this soup! It can also be served as an appetizer.*

2 PORTIONS OR 4 SMALL PORTIONS

- 1 quart (1 liter) fresh False Saffron Milk Caps or 7 oz (200 g) frozen
- butter for frying
- ½ tbsp mushroom flour (see p. 17)
- ½ cup (100 ml) water
- ½ cup (100 ml) milk
- ¼ cup (50 ml) whipping cream
- 1 tbsp concentrated vegetable or chicken stock, or a strong broth
- 2 oz (40 g) grated Västerbotten cheese (can be purchased in specialty stores or online, or substitute with your favorite aged cheese)
- ¾–1 inch (2–3 cm) leek, finely sliced
- salt and pepper

Fry the mushrooms in butter to give them some color. Keep a few nice pieces for serving and place the rest in a saucepan. Sprinkle mushroom flour on top and pour the water, milk, cream, and stock on top. Cover and cook for 10–15 minutes.

Add the cheese and let it melt. Then, blend the soup. Pour into four small bowls (or two large ones) and serve with the fried False Saffron Milk Caps and some finely sliced leek.

# BREDBERG'S SOUP

*Monica Svensson is a mushroom expert who has experimented to create this Matsutake soup recipe. She got some help from her grandson, so the soup is named after him.*

4 PORTIONS OR 8 SMALL PORTIONS

- 1¾ oz (50 g) dried Matsutake mushrooms
- 2 slices of bacon
- 1 bunch of Thai basil or cilantro
- 1 tbsp butter
- 1 garlic clove, finely chopped
- 2½ cups (600 ml) milk
- 1¼ cups (300 ml) cream
- ⅔ cup (150 ml) crème fraîche or sour cream
- 2 tbsp concentrated veal stock
- 1 tsp Dijon mustard
- ⅓ lemon, zest and juice

Soak the dried mushrooms in tepid water for a few hours. The water ought to cover the mushrooms the whole time, so add more if the water gets absorbed.

Slice the bacon thinly and fry until crispy, retaining the fat. Remove the leaves from the basil or cilantro; these will be used at the end. Finely chop the stalks.

Pour the mushrooms, together with the water they have soaked in, into a saucepan and cook until the liquid is absorbed. Add the butter and "sweat" the mushrooms for about 10 minutes over low heat. Add the garlic at the end.

Add milk, cream, crème fraîche, stock, and the stalks from the herbs, and cook for about 20 minutes.

Add the mustard, the lemon zest and juice, half the bacon, and the fat from frying it. Blend the soup; otherwise, if the mushroom pieces are too big, they can be somewhat chewy.

This soup tastes better if you let it rest for a while. Heat it up before serving and sprinkle the rest of the bacon bits and the roughly chopped basil or cilantro on top.

Matsutake mushrooms have a very special, slightly flowery taste, and in this soup it really comes into its own. If you can't find this particular mushroom, it can be substituted with 1 quart (1 liter) of fresh Shiitake mushrooms, which obviously don't need to be soaked. Cut the Shiitake into small pieces, fry in the butter, and then follow the recipe.

# MUSHROOM BURGERS

*Lovely mushroom patties that can be flavored
in a variety of ways.*

4 PORTIONS

- 1 quart (1 liter) frozen mushrooms or
  2 quarts (2 liters) fresh mushrooms,
  chopped into pieces
- 2 cups (500 ml) stock, made from a bouillon
  cube
- 2 tbsp grated onion
- olive oil or canola oil
- 3½ tbsp (50 ml) mushroom flour (see p. 17)
- ¼ cup (50 ml) breadcrumbs
- 2 tbsp potato flour
- ¼ cup (50 ml) cream
- 1 egg
- 1 tsp Dijon mustard
- sesame seeds, for breading
- salt and pepper

Place the fresh or dried mushrooms in the
boiling stock and cook for 15 minutes. Remove
the stock, and save it to make soups or sauces
if you so desire; it can easily be frozen. Fry the
onion in some oil. Place the cooled mushrooms and onion in a food processor and
finely blend. Add mushroom flour, breadcrumbs, potato flour, cream, egg, and mustard.

Add salt and pepper to taste. Mix and let rest
for about 10 minutes.

Test fry a small piece to see if the mixture
stays firm and to test the taste of the seasoning. If it falls apart, add some more potato
flour. Form into small patties and coat in the
sesame seeds. Fry in oil over medium heat
until cooked through.

Serve with a slice of lemon or lime.

Other flavorings: 1 fresh garlic clove and
4 tbsp (50 ml) chopped parsley. Sauce
suggestion: Fry a clove of crushed garlic and a
finely chopped chili in 2 tbsp olive oil over low
heat. Add ½–¾ cup (100–200 g) chopped
tomatoes and cook, adding salt to taste.

Take some Crab Brittlegills and Weeping Milk
Cap and add 2 tbsp chopped dill and 1 tbsp
lime juice to give it a "fishy" feel. Serve with a
white wine sauce, with or without mushrooms; see page 85.

# RISOTTO

*The first time I tried risotto, which was late in life, I thought it was the best thing I had ever tasted! Celebrity chef Mathias Dahlgren was also seated at the table, and everyone's eyes were on him. "A bit too much truffle oil," he exclaimed. "Aha!" I thought. "Truffle oil." I duly made a risotto on my return home. These days I tend to leave out the truffle oil, but it definitely elevates the flavor of the dish.*

4 PORTIONS

- 1 quart (1 liter) fresh mushrooms
- 2–3 tbsp canola oil
- 1 yellow onion or 2 shallots, finely chopped
- 1⅔ cups (400 ml) Arborio rice
- ¾ cup (200 ml) white wine or cooking wine
- 1 tbsp mushroom flour (optional), see p. 17
- 4½ cups (1 liter) water
- 2 bouillon cubes, chicken, mushroom, or vegetable
- ½ cup (100 ml) grated Parmesan
- salt and pepper

Cut the mushrooms into pieces. Heat the oil in a saucepan and fry the mushrooms and onion until the onion turns translucent.

Add the rice and fry it, but avoid giving it color. Add the wine, and if desired, mushroom flour. Boil the water in a separate saucepan and add the bouillon cubes. Add the stock to the rice, a little at a time, stirring continuously until the rice is ready, about 20–30 minutes. The rice should cook over a low heat.

Add Parmesan and season with salt and pepper.

Serve.

Risotto works with most things: meat, poultry, fish, cooked vegetables, or just a salad. I often use mushroom flour or crumble in some dried mushrooms that I add after the wine. As it absorbs liquid, you may need to use more stock.

If you want it to have an even stronger mushroom taste, you can, as mentioned, add some truffle oil.

If I make rice pudding over Christmas and have some leftover rice, I'll often use it to make risotto.

# BREADED PARASOL MUSHROOMS

*Sometimes you can find vast amounts of Parasol mushrooms. If this is the case, serve some breaded Parasol mushrooms and have your guests guess what they are eating—they may not imagine it's a mushroom!*

4 PORTIONS

- 4 large Parasol Mushroom caps, or the equivalent in smaller caps
- ¼ cup (50 ml) lemon juice
- 2 eggs
- 2 tbsp water
- 1¼ cups (300 ml) breadcrumbs
- 1 tsp salt
- pinch of pepper
- approx. ¾ cups (200 ml) wheat flour
- ¾ cup (200 ml) canola oil

*To serve:*
- lemon slices
- capers

Flat Parasol caps can be left whole. If they are domed, it's better to cut them in half or quarters to make them easier to fry. Brush some lemon juice on the caps. Whisk together eggs and water in a wide, deep bowl. Mix the breadcrumbs with salt and pepper.

Roll the caps in the flour, then the eggs, and finally the breadcrumbs. Fry them in a frying pan in plenty of oil until golden brown.

Serve freshly fried with lemon slices and capers. Mashed potatoes and salad make great accompaniments.

Try placing a slice of cheese between two caps, or even a slice of cheese and a slice of smoked ham. Secure with a toothpick so they don't fall apart when you fry them.

Instead of brushing the caps with lemon, you can use milk.

# PORCINI CARBONARA

*Pasta carbonara is a great dish, but why not try a vegetarian version?*

4 PORTIONS

- 11 oz (300 g) pasta
- 1 quart (1 liter) fresh, sliced porcini
- 1–2 tbsp canola or olive oil for frying
- ½ onion, finely chopped
- 4 egg yolks
- ¼ cup (50 ml) water or cream
- salt and pepper

*To serve:*
- ¾ cup (200 ml) grated Parmesan
- salad

Boil the pasta.

Fry the mushrooms in some oil, add the onion, and fry until the mushrooms get a bit of color and the onion is tender.

Mix the egg yolks and water or cream with the mushrooms. Pour over the drained pasta and stir. Season with salt and pepper, and serve with the grated Parmesan, or another cheese, and a salad.

If you only have a small amount of Porcini, you can mix them with other Boletales, False Saffron Milk Caps, or a mixture of mushrooms. You can also try the dish with Trumpet Chanterelles and fry them together with a slice of bacon (although in this case it will no longer be vegetarian).

# QUINOA AND MUSHROOM SALAD

*My grandmother always planted fava beans together, and I remember the excitement of opening the large, fuzzy pods and plucking out the beans. This is a great "harvest salad"; in addition, it is both vegetarian and gluten free.*

4 PORTIONS

- 1 quart (1 liter) fresh mixed mushrooms
- 4 tbsp vinegar
- 4 tbsp oil
- 4 tbsp water
- 1 tsp salt
- 1 pinch coarsely ground black pepper
- 3½ oz (100 g) cooked fava beans or 3½ oz (100 g) frozen soy beans
- 3 average-sized carrots
- 3½ oz (100 g) sugar snap peas
- ½ red onion, chopped or finely sliced
- 1⅔ cup (400 ml) quinoa
- 3⅓ cups (800 ml) water or vegetable stock

*Sauce:*
- ¾ cup (200 ml) yogurt
- 2 tbsp freshly chopped herbs
- salt
- 1 garlic clove, optional
- 2 tsp olive oil for serving

Cut the mushrooms into large chunks; small mushrooms can be left whole. Boil in plenty of salted water for 10–15 minutes.

Drain the water. Mix vinegar, oil, water, salt, and black pepper and bring to a boil. Add the mushrooms and let them simmer slowly for ten minutes.

Shell the beans and place them in boiling water; when they float to the top, they are ready. Discard the water and peel off the chewy outer casing. Peel the carrots and divide them into large chunks and blanch in some salty water. Add the sugar snap peas to the water when there's a minute left.

Mix all the ingredients for the sauce (except the oil).

Cook the quinoa in water or vegetable stock according to the instructions and stir the hot mushroom mixture into the quinoa, so that it is evenly combined. Add the vegetables and stir. Serve the salad warm, room temperature, or cold together with the sauce. Pour the oil over the sauce just before serving.

If you like, you can swap the quinoa for couscous, but in this case then it will no longer be a gluten–free dish.

# ROOT VEGETABLE GRATIN WITH GYPSY MUSHROOM

*Root vegetables and mushrooms work well together. Serve the gratin as a stand-alone dish or together with any type of meat or spicy sausage.*

4–6 PORTIONS

- 1½ quart (1½ liters) thinly sliced Gypsy mushrooms
- butter or oil for frying
- 3 yellow onions, thinly sliced
- 7 oz (200 g) rutabaga
- 7 oz (200 g) carrots
- 3½ oz (100 g) parsnips
- 3½ oz (100 g) celeriac
- 7 oz (200 g) kohlrabi
- 1¼ cup (300 ml) cream
- ½ cup (100 ml) mushroom or vegetable stock
- 1½ tsp salt
- ¼ tsp pepper
- 1 tbsp fresh thyme, chopped, or 1 tsp dried
- ½ cup (50 ml) grated cheese

Fry the mushrooms in butter or oil until the liquid is absorbed and the mushrooms have gotten a bit of color. Fry the onion with the mushrooms.

Thinly slice the root vegetables, preferably in a food processor.

Combine the cream and stock in a nonstick saucepan, bring to a boil, and add the vegetables, cooking them slowly under a lid until they soften. Add salt and pepper. Add more water if it becomes too dry. Drain the vegetables and keep the creamy stock.

Layer the vegetables, mushrooms, onions, and herbs in a buttered, ovenproof dish. Pour the cream stock on top and sprinkle with grated cheese.

Cook in the oven at 400°F (200°C) until the vegetables are soft, for about 30 minutes. Reduce the temperature to 350°F (175°C) if you think the gratin is done before the vegetables are cooked through.

The gratin also works well with other mushrooms, for example Trumpet Chanterelles, store-bought Button mushrooms, or a mixture of mushrooms.

Substitute the cream and stock for ½ cup (100 ml) oil and 1¼ cup (300 ml) stock (reduce the salt in the recipe). Skip the cheese and use oil instead of butter, and the gratin is suitable for vegans!

# MUSHROOM DUMPLINGS

40 DUMPLINGS

*Dough:*
- ⅓ oz (10 g) active dry yeast
- 1 cup (250 ml) lukewarm water
- 3⅓ cups (500 ml) wheat flour (1 lb/500 g)

*Filling:*
- 1 quart (1 liter) fresh or 10½ oz (300 g) frozen mushrooms
- 10½ oz (300 g) fresh white cabbage, finely grated
- oil for frying
- 1 garlic clove, finely chopped
- ¾ inch (2 cm) fresh ginger, grated
- 3 tbsp Japanese soy sauce
- 2 tbsp concentrated vegetable or chicken stock
- ½ tbsp lime juice or vinegar
- ½ tsp cane sugar
- ½ inch (1 cm) red chili, shredded, or ½ tsp sambal oelek
- 1 tsp fresh cilantro, chopped
- 1½–2 tbsp sesame oil

Dissolve the yeast in the water and add the flour a little at a time while working it. Knead the dough and then leave it to rise under a kitchen towel for about 30 minutes. Finely chop the mushrooms and fry them in the oil until the liquid has been absorbed. Fry the cabbage in a little oil until it starts to reduce in size. Add the mushrooms, garlic, ginger, soy, stock, lime, cane sugar, and chili and cook until the cabbage is soft and most of the liquid is absorbed.

Roll out the dough and divide into 40 pieces. Make a small ball from each piece and roll out until they are about 4 inches (10 cm) in diameter, and place 1 tbsp of the filling on each one. Moisten the edges with a little water and press them into dumplings, pinching the edges together to seal them. Steam in a steamer for about 15 minutes. Alternately, place a large colander over a pan of boiling water and cover with a folded towel or a lid and cook for about 15 minutes. Make sure the dumplings do not touch, as they will stick together.

Serve with soy sauce.

If your oven has a steam function, the dumplings can be cooked in the oven. You can also cook them in water, but they won't turn out as well. The parcels can also be fried in oil to give them some color. Then you can add some water, cover, and steam them for 5 minutes.

Swap some or all of the mushrooms for Oyster mushrooms or Shiitake mushrooms. Shiitakes have a strong taste, so you don't need as much. Wonton wrappers can be purchased in most Asian groceries if you don't want to make the dough at home.

# YELLOW FOOT, CHANTERELLE, AND LECCINUM PASTA

*A quick and easy pasta that tastes fantastic.*

4 PORTIONS

- 11 oz (300 g) pasta
- 1½ quart (1½ liter) fresh Yellow Foot, Chanterelles, and Leccinum
- 8–10 cherry tomatoes
- ¼ cup (50 ml) olive or canola oil
- 1–2 garlic cloves, thinly sliced
- ½ –¾ inches (1–2 cm) red chili, finely shredded
- thyme and parsley, chopped
- salt and coarsely ground pepper

Cook the pasta according to the instructions on the packaging.

Cut the mushrooms into large pieces. Chop the tomatoes in half and fry them at a high heat for a few minutes. Reduce the heat and add the mushrooms; cook until they get some color, then add garlic and chili, and fry for a few more minutes. Season with salt and lots of pepper, and sprinkle thyme and parsley on top.

Serve the mushroom mixture with the warm pasta, preferably with grated cheese on top and a salad.

Ketchup tastes great as an accompaniment. Instead of fresh tomatoes, you can drain ½ cup (100 ml) of canned, chopped tomatoes and fry them in oil.

If you want to add some protein, you can add a fried egg to each portion.

# WEEPING MILK CAP BLINIS WITH DILL

4 PORTIONS

*Blinis:*
- 2 eggs
- approx. ½ oz (12½ g) active dry yeast
- 2 cups (500 ml) milk
- ¾ cup + 1 tbsp (200 ml) buckwheat flour
- ¾ cup + 1 tbsp (200 ml) wheat flour
- 1 tsp salt
- 3½ tbsp (50 g) butter, plus extra for frying

*Weeping Milk Caps with dill:*
- 3⅓ cups (800 ml) fresh Crab Brittlegills and 1 Weeping Milk Cap
- 2 tbsp butter
- 1 red onion, chopped
- ¾ cup (200 g) crème fraîche or sour cream
- 1 bunch of dill, chopped
- salt and pepper

*To serve:*
- 1 red onion, cut into thin rings
- dill
- lemon slices

Break the eggs and separate the yolks from the whites. Dissolve the yeast in the warm milk, and add the buckwheat and wheat flour a little at a time while whisking. Whisk the batter until it's smooth and free of any lumps. Add salt and the egg yolks, cover the bowl, and leave the batter to stand for an hour at room temperature.

Melt the butter and let it cool. Whisk the egg whites to form a stiff foam and gently fold the butter and egg whites into the batter just before cooking.

Fry the blinis on both sides in a pancake/blini pan over medium heat—use a bit of butter, if you wish. Alternatively, use a regular frying pan and place three to four spoonfuls of batter in the pan to make the blinis.

Dice the mushrooms and place in a saucepan; cook them in their own juices until the liquid is absorbed. Add butter and fry together with half of the red onion. Add the crème fraîche or sour cream and cook together while stirring. Add the dill and the rest of the onion and season with salt and pepper.

Serve the blinis with red onion, dill, and lemon slices.

Crab Brittlegills can be swapped for other Russula or Leccinum.

The Milk Cap salad on page 117 pairs well with this dish.

Buckwheat flour is gluten free, so if you swap that for the wheat flour, the blinis will be gluten free.

# MUSHROOM HASH

*During the Second World War, it was common to use Sheep Polypore or Wood Hedgehog as a substitute for meat. The mushrooms were fried and eaten as a steak, or made into a hash.*

4 PORTIONS

- 4–5 (¾ lb/400 g) average-sized potatoes
- 3 quarts (3 liters) fresh Wood Hedgehog or Sheep Polypore
- 2 yellow onions, chopped
- 3 tbsp butter
- 3½ tbsp (50 ml) chopped parsley
- salt and black pepper

*To serve:*
- 4 fried eggs
- pickled beetroots

Peel and dice the potatoes. Place in salted, boiling water and cook a few minutes before straining. They should still feel quite solid.

Cut the mushrooms into cubes and fry together with the onions in half of the butter, so they get some color.

Fry the potatoes in the remaining butter until they are cooked through and get some color. Add the mushrooms and onions to the potato and stir, heating the mixture through. Season to taste with salt and pepper, and sprinkle with parsley.

Serve with eggs and beetroots.

If you have any leftover sausage or meat, you can chop it up and add it to the dish. In this case, use fewer mushrooms.

# PORCINI FOCCACIA

*You can try this dish with other Boletales, but the mushrooms can't be sliced too thin, as they burn easily.*

- 2–3 fresh, average-sized Porcini
- olive oil
- 2–3 garlic cloves, thinly sliced
- fresh herbs, such as sage, rosemary, or thyme
- 2 tbsp olive oil
- sea salt flakes and pepper

- approx. ½ oz (12½ g) active dry yeast
- 1⅓ cups (300 ml) water
- 1 tsp salt
- 1 tsp honey, optional
- 2 tbsp olive oil
- 3 cups (700 ml) bread flour

*Gluten-free dough:*
- approx. ½ oz (12½ g) active dry yeast
- 1 tsp honey
- ¼ cup (50 ml) warm water
- 3 cups + 1½ tbsp (750 ml) light, gluten-free flour mix
- 3½ tbsp (50 ml) powdered milk
- ½ tbsp psyllium husk
- 1 tsp salt
- 1 tsp baking soda
- 2 cups (500 ml) yogurt
- 2 tbsp olive oil
- 1 egg

Slice the mushrooms into slices that are ¼ inch (½ cm) thick. Fry them in oil until the liquid is absorbed and the mushrooms get some color. Add the garlic when there are a few minutes remaining. Add salt and pepper and let cool.

Dissolve the yeast in the water. Add salt and, if you like, some honey, as well as the olive oil. Add flour a little at a time and work the dough for at least 5 minutes if you are using a mixer; if kneading by hand, double the time. The dough should be fairly loose. Cover with a kitchen towel and let it rise for 40 minutes.

Grease a pan or line with parchment paper and, with floured hands, press the dough onto the pan. Let it rise under a towel for 30 minutes.

Preheat the oven to 475°F (250°C). Distribute the mushrooms, garlic, and herbs on the dough, pressing down with your fingers to make sure they stick. Drizzle some olive oil on top and sprinkle the sea salt over the dough. Place the bread in the oven and immediately decrease the temperature to 400°F (200°C). Bake for 25–30 minutes.

*Gluten-free dough:*
Dissolve the yeast and honey in the water and mix together all the dry ingredients. Warm the yogurt and add the oil and the egg. Pour the wet ingredients into the flour and knead the dough for at least 5 minutes using a mixer. Press the dough onto a greased pan and let it rise under a kitchen towel for 30–40 minutes. Follow the instructions above and then bake at 425°F (225°C) for about 20 minutes.

# MUSHROOM QUESADILLA

*Quesadillas can be served as a snack, as an accompaniment to drinks, or at a picnic.*

MAKES 4

- 1 quart (1 liter) fresh or 1½ cups (300 ml) frozen mushrooms
- oil for frying
- 1 cooked and peeled cold potato
- 2 garlic cloves, sliced
- 2 red onions, chopped
- ¾ cup (200 ml) grated cheese
- 1 tsp fresh lemon or lime juice
- 2 tbsp chopped parsley
- 1 tbsp oil
- 8 small tortillas
- 1 egg
- salt and pepper

Quickly fry the fresh mushrooms until all the liquid has evaporated. Fry the fresh or frozen mushrooms in oil to brown them. Add salt. Mash the potato and mix in the onion, cheese, lime juice, parsley, and mushrooms, and season with salt and pepper.

Brush the tortillas with a whisked egg on one side. Place the potato mixture on 4 of the tortillas and place the other 4 on top—the brushed sides should be on the inside. Press along the edges and fry on both sides in a dry frying pan. The tortillas need to be heated through so the cheese melts.

Serve hot or cold, whole, or in smaller pieces.

# OVEN-BAKED MUSHROOM OMELET

When I was young and celebrated Christmas with my paternal grandparents, my grandmother always made a mushroom omelet with Chanterelles specially for me. My mother-in-law, Pelle's mother, also always served a mushroom omelet on the Christmas table, and now we carry on this tradition. We often buy fresh Button mushrooms and mix them with our own dried mushrooms.

4 PORTIONS

Mushroom mixture:
- 1 quart (1 liter) fresh mushrooms, 1¼–1⅔ cups (300–400 ml) precooked mushrooms, or 1 oz (30 g) dried
- 2 tbsp butter
- 2 tbsp wheat flour
- ⅔ cup (150 ml) water
- ⅔ cup (150 ml) cream
- salt and pepper

Oven-baked omelet:
- 1⅔ cup (400 ml) milk
- 6 eggs
- 1 tsp salt

Dried mushrooms need to soak; fresh or pre-cooked mushrooms can be placed in a saucepan and cooked in their own juices until most of the liquid is absorbed. Add some butter and fry the mushrooms, adding flour while stirring. Dilute with the water, and then add the cream. Let the mushrooms simmer slowly for at least 15 minutes and then add salt and pepper to taste.

Heat the milk for the omelet and let it cool. Whisk the milk, eggs, and salt and pour into a greased, ovenproof dish. Bake in the center of the oven at 400°F (200°) for about 20 minutes or until the omelet is cooked through. Pour the mushroom mixture on top.

Serve with a salad or some bread as a main course, or serve it as part of a buffet.

A mushroom mixture like the one above can be used in a variety of ways. It can be served with an omelet, placed on a sandwich and grilled, baked into custards or quiche and used as side dishes for meat and fish, or it can be diluted with some jus to make a sauce. In the same way that Pelle's mushroom soup can be made fancier, you can enhance this dish with wine or cognac, and the cream can be swapped for crème fraîche.

# MUSHROOM EGG SANDWICH

*The Velvet Bolete isn't especially exciting when fresh, but it has a great taste when dried.*

4 PORTIONS

*Creamy mushroom mixture:*
- approx. ½ oz (15 g) dried Velvet Bolete, or 1 quart (1 liter) fresh mushrooms of any sort
- 2 tbsp butter
- ½ cup (100 ml) water for soaking
- 3 tbsp wheat flour
- ⅔ cup (150 ml) milk
- ⅔ cup (150 ml) cream
- rosemary, optional
- salt and pepper

- 4 hard-blanched eggs
- 8 slices of bread
- ¾ cup (200 ml) grated Västerbotten cheese (can be bought in specialty stores or online, or substitute with your favorite aged cheese)

Crumble the dried Velvet Bolete and soak for about 20 minutes in warm water. Drain and keep the water. Melt the butter and fry the mushrooms at a low heat. You can dilute this with the water you've saved if it starts to get too dry. Add the rest of the saved water and cook for a few minutes. Dilute the flour in some of the milk and pour the rest of the milk and cream onto the mushrooms; bring to a boil. Thicken with the milk and flour mixture and season to taste with salt, pepper, and a bit of rosemary, if you like.

Peel the eggs, and slice and distribute them across 4 slices of bread. Place the mushroom mixture on top and sprinkle with some grated cheese. Bake for about 5–10 minutes at 450°F (225°C) or until the cheese starts to brown.

Serve with a salad and you have a complete meal.

This mushroom mix can be created from almost any mushrooms you like, including mixed mushrooms, Button mushrooms, False Saffron Milk Caps, Trumpet Chanterelles, Chanterelles, or Porcini. Use mushrooms you already have or buy canned or fresh ones at the store.

You can make several small appetizer sandwiches by punching out circles of bread with a cookie cutter or cutting the bread into squares and removing the crusts.

# OMELET WITH ENOKITAKE AND VEGETABLES

*This is really quick food! Great for when you feel famished and need to eat quickly, or if someone else turns up hungry at your door. It's also good if you have an unexpected vegetarian guest at dinner!*

1 PORTION

- ⅓ cup (25 g) fresh Enokitake, or another variety
- a dash of sesame oil, optional
- 1 tsp canola oil
- 1 pinch garam masala or curry powder
- ½ carrot, sliced
- ¾ inch (2 cm) leeks, sliced
- 2–3 strips of red pepper
- 4–5 goosefoot leaves, optional
- ½ tbsp fresh cilantro, chopped
- a pinch of salt
- 2 eggs
- black pepper

Fry the mushroom in a dry frying pan until all the liquid is absorbed. Add oil and garam masala and then the carrot, leek, and pepper. Fry until the vegetables start to soften. Add the goosefoot, cilantro, and salt. Whisk the eggs and pour over the mushrooms and vegetables. Fry the omelet over low heat and, when it starts to set on top, flip it over and fry for a further few minutes. Serve.

Enokitake can be bought at Asian grocery stores and looks like spaghetti with a little knob. You can also find these growing wild. You can also use another mushroom, for example, the Trumpet Chanterelle. Dried mushrooms can also be used, but they need to be soaked first.

You can use most vegetables for this dish, such as onion instead of leek. Goosefoot is a weed that grows in our garden, but spinach or chard can also be used.

If you just want to use mushrooms and egg, it will be just as delicious; simply use a few more mushrooms.

# MUSHROOM PIE WITH MOZZARELLA AND CHARD

*Chard with mushroom is a match made in heaven, found here in a pie with crème fraîche, mozzarella, and tomatoes.*

4 PORTIONS

*For the pie:*
- approx. 2 cups (500 ml) wheat flour
- 7 oz (200 g) butter
- ½ tsp salt
- ¼ cup (50 ml) water
- 1 small egg
- ½ tsp white vinegar

*For the filling:*
- 1 quart (1 liter) fresh mushrooms, in pieces
- butter or oil for frying
- 1 onion (red or yellow), chopped
- 10 oz (300 g) fresh chard or spinach
- ¾ cup (200 g) crème fraîche or sour cream
- 3 eggs
- 4½ oz (125 g) mozzarella
- 7–8 cherry tomatoes, divided
- salt and pepper

Chop together the flour, butter, and salt to combine. Make a dent in the center of the flour and butter mix. Combine water, egg, and vinegar and pour into the dent, then mix everything together quickly and leave it in the fridge for at least 30 minutes. Prepare the filling while you wait.

Fry the mushrooms until the liquid has evaporated and add butter or oil. Brown the mushrooms and then add the onion. Fry until the onion becomes translucent. Roughly chop the chard and fry it with the onions for a while, then remove from the heat. Combine the crème fraîche and eggs and then mix together with the mushrooms and chard. Add salt and pepper to taste.

Roll out the dough and place in a greased pan. Prick the dough a few times and precook in the oven for 10 minutes at 450°F (225°C), then reduce the heat to 400°F (200°C). Pour in the mixture and place slices of mozzarella and tomato on top. Bake at the bottom of the oven for 30 minutes.

Mixed mushrooms, Boletales, Russula, Chanterelles, Trumpet Chanterelles—any mushroom can be used for this dish.

# VEGETABLE PIE WITH MUSHROOMS

*Mushroom pies make a great addition to a buffet. They complement both fish and meat, or can be eaten with a salad for a vegetarian meal.*

4 PORTIONS

*For the pie:*
- approx. 2 cups (500 ml) wheat flour
- 7 oz (200 g) butter
- ½ tsp salt
- ¼ cup (50 ml) water
- 1 small egg
- ½ tsp white vinegar

*For the filling:*
- 1 quart (1 liter) fresh mushrooms, in pieces
- 1 yellow onion, finely chopped
- 2 leeks, chopped
- 1 large carrot, roughly grated
- butter or oil for frying
- ¾ cup (200 ml) crème fraîche or sour cream
- 2 eggs
- salt and pepper

Chop together flour, butter, and salt to combine. Make a dent in the flour and butter mixture. Combine water, egg, and vinegar and pour into the dent, then mix everything together quickly and place in the fridge for at least 30 minutes. Prepare the filling while you wait.

Fry the mushroom, onion, and carrot in the butter and remove from the heat. Combine the crème fraîche and egg and then combine with the mushroom and vegetables.

Roll out the dough and place in a greased pan. Prick the bottom a few times and precook in the oven for 10 minutes at 450°F (225°C), then reduce the heat to 400°F (200°C). Pour in the mixture and place slices of mozzarella and tomato on top. Bake at the bottom of the oven for 30 minutes.

Most mushrooms can be used for this dish, and preferably use a mixture of mushrooms. I sometimes use Wood Hedgehogs and add a pinch of curry when frying.

I've even made a vegan pie. Simply swap the butter in the dough with a vegan-friendly margarine and substitute the crème fraîche with a soy product that you can dilute with 2 tsp cornstarch to ensure the mixture sets.

# POT PIE

*Here are some small, personal pies that can be served as a starter or a side. They work well with spicy sausages, pork, or chicken.*

4 PORTIONS

- 1 quart (1 liter) fresh mushrooms
- oil for frying
- 1 small yellow onion, chopped
- 3½ oz (100 g) rutabaga, diced
- 3½ oz (100 g) parsnip, diced
- 3½ oz (100 g) potato, diced
- 3½ oz (100 g) sweet potato, diced
- 1¾ oz (50 g) celeriac, diced
- ½ cup (100 ml) water
- 1 tsp concentrated vegetable or chicken stock
- 1 tsp salt
- a pinch of pepper
- 2 tbsp cream
- ¼–½ cup (50–100 ml) peas or chopped sugar snap peas

- 2 frozen puff pastry sheets
- 1 whisked egg for brushing

Cut the mushrooms into cubes. Place in a frying pan and fry until the liquid is absorbed. Add the oil and brown the mushrooms. Add the onion and fry with the mushrooms until it softens. Set aside. The diced root vegetables should amount to roughly 3½ cups (800 ml). Fry them in oil to give them some color. Place the root vegetables and mushrooms in a saucepan, pour in the water and stock, and add salt and pepper. Cover and boil until almost cooked through, then add the cream and let the vegetables and cream cook together uncovered. Season to taste. Add the peas and remove the pan from the heat.

Fill four small, ovenproof ramekins with the mushroom and vegetable mixture. Preheat the oven to 450°F (225°C). Roll out the dough and make four circles that are slightly larger than the ramekins. Place on top to serve as lids and then brush with the egg. Bake until the dough has risen and is a nice, golden color.

If you have some leftover cooked chicken, you can use it with this dish to make chicken pot pie. It doesn't take much to turn this into a full meal. If you want to serve the pies as a starter, you can use eight smaller ramekins. If you don't have sweet potato, simply increase the amount of the other vegetables. However, don't use more celeriac, as it has a strong taste and can easily overpower the dish.

# EVA LOODH'S PEACH CHICKEN

*Eva Loodh is one of Sweden's most prominent mushroom experts and she gave us this recipe for a mild but flavorful chicken stew. We have a peach tree in our yard and all the peaches seem to ripen at once, right in the middle of the mushroom season. It's great to be able to use them when cooking.*

4 PORTIONS

- 1 quart (1 liter) fresh mushrooms, preferably Boletales
- butter and oil for frying

*For the breading:*
- 3½ tbsp (50 ml) cornstarch
- 1 tsp mushroom flour (see p. 17)
- ¼ tsp white pepper
- ¼ tsp cayenne pepper
- ¼ tsp allspice
- ¼ tsp black pepper
- ¼ tsp curry powder
- 1 tsp salt

- 1½ lb (600 g) chicken breast, cut into strips
- 2 garlic cloves, crushed
- 5 peaches
- ¾ cup (200 ml) water
- ¾ cup (200 ml) milk
- ¾ cup (200 g) cream
- 2–3 chicken bouillon cubes

Fry the mushrooms in butter and oil until they start to brown. Set aside. Mix all the ingredients for the breading in a bag and place the chicken strips into it, shaking it so that all the pieces are coated. Fry the chicken in butter and oil until golden brown. Place the chicken and mushrooms in a deep pan and add the garlic.

Peel the peaches with a knife. Cut them into wedges and place them in the pan. Pour the water on top and cook for about 10 minutes. Add the milk and cream and cook until the chicken is done and the sauce has a creamy consistency. Serve with rice or potatoes and a salad.

Dried, frozen, or store-bought mushrooms also work well. For more information see the chapter on cooking mushrooms.

# CHICKEN WITH BLACK MOREL

*Black morels do not need to be blanched before using. In Sweden and Finland, some people will eat the poisonous False Morel after boiling it twice. Our advice, however, is to not eat False Morels at all.*

4 PORTIONS

- 4 fresh Black Morels
- oil for frying
- 4 chicken breasts
- ¼ cup (50 ml) potato flour

*For the sauce:*
- ½ cup (100 ml) Japanese soy sauce
- ½ cup (100 ml) water or chicken stock
- 1 tbsp mirin or 1 tsp sugar
- 1 tsp vinegar
- ¾ inch (2 cm) red chili, thinly sliced
- 1–2 garlic cloves
- ¾ inch (2 cm) fresh ginger, grated

Slice the Black Morels and fry them in oil. Set aside. Combine the sauce in a saucepan that will be big enough to fit the chicken.

Cut the chicken into smaller pieces and bread them in the potato flour. Fry them in the oil but do not brown them. Place the chicken and mushrooms in the sauce and cook until the chicken is cooked through. Serve with rice and stir-fried vegetables.

Black Trumpets, Trumpet Chanterelles, Yellow Foot, or Shiitake also work well for this dish, and 2 cups (150 g) of mushrooms will be enough. Instead of making the sauce yourself, you can use ¾ cup (200 ml) readymade teriyaki sauce.

# SALMON DOLMAS WITH BLACK TRUMPETS

*Black Trumpets and salmon wrapped in cabbage leaves are a slightly fancier version of the classic dolma.*

4 PORTIONS

- ½ cup (20 g) dried Black Trumpet or 2 cups (½ liter) fresh
- butter for frying
- 1 whole savoy cabbage
- salt
- 1 lb (500 g) fresh or frozen salmon
- ¾ inch (2 cm) fresh ginger, grated
- 2 shallots, chopped
- 1 lime, juice
- 2 tsp potato flour
- 1 tsp salt
- pepper, optional

Soak the dried mushrooms in warm water until they soften. Discard the water and slowly fry the soaked or fresh mushrooms in butter. Add a little water if it seems too dry. Let cool.

Cut off the end of the cabbage. Boil plenty of lightly salted water in a pot big enough to fit the whole cabbage. Place the cabbage in the pot. Quickly remove it and peel off the leaves that have softened. Repeat the process until the leaves are too small to use. Let the leaves cool.

Thaw the frozen salmon; cut into small pieces and place in a bowl. Combine the ginger and onion with the salmon, lime juice, potato flour, 1 tsp salt, and a dash of pepper, if you like. Add the Black Trumpets and let cool.

Preheat the oven to 450°F (225°C). Place about 1 tbsp of the salmon mixture on each cabbage leave and fold together to make the dolmas. Place them close together in a greased, ovenproof dish and brush with melted butter. Place in the oven for about 20 minutes.

Serve with rice, Japanese soy sauce, or lightly cooked carrots and sugar snaps, or with a white wine sauce (see page 85) and potatoes.

# COD AND WHITE WINE SAUCE WITH MUSHROOMS

*Mushrooms work well with most foods, even fish—no matter whether it is fried, grilled, or blanched. You can experiment with different types of fish and mushrooms.*

4 PORTIONS

- 1¼ cup (300 ml) fresh mushrooms
- 2 shallots, finely chopped
- butter for frying
- ¾ cup (200 ml) fish stock
- 1½ tbsp wheat flour
- ½ cup (100 ml) dry white wine
- ½ cup (100 ml) cream
- 1¼ lb (600 g) fillet of cod
- salt and white pepper

*To serve:*
- blanched carrots
- blanched sugar snap peas
- dill
- slices of lemon or lime

Finely chop the mushrooms. Fry the mushrooms and shallots slowly in butter until the shallots become translucent and then add the stock. Combine the flour and wine and add to the sauce using a whisk. Bring to a boil. Add the cream and let it simmer for about 5 minutes. Season to taste with salt and pepper.

Fry or grill the fish, which should be cut to individual portion sizes, and season with salt and pepper.

Serve with the sauce, carrots, and sugar snaps. Garnish with the dill and lemon or lime.

This sauce works well with other fish dishes. With salmon, it's good to use flavorful mushrooms, such as like Black Trumpet, Fairy Ring mushrooms, and Trumpet Chanterelles. White fish works well with Russula, Crab Brittlegill, and Weeping Milk Cap.

# LOBSTER AU GRATIN

*We have celebrated many a New Year's Eve with our neighbors. We usually go to a pot luck dinner, and we'll often bring this starter. It always looks impressive when it's served straight out of the lobster shell. My sister-in-law Gunilla also makes this at New Year's Eve, but she places her mixture in scallop shells, just like Grandma Signe used to do.*

4 PORTIONS

- 2 frozen lobsters
- 3¼ cup (800 ml) sliced, fresh Button mushrooms or Entire Russula
- 4 tbsp butter
- 2 tbsp wheat flour
- 1⅔ cup (400 ml) milk or half-and-half
- ¾ cup (200 ml) grated cheese
- 1½ tbsp cognac
- salt and pepper

Thaw the lobsters overnight in the fridge. Divide them and remove the tails. Carefully crack the claws so that they remain whole and can be filled with some of the mixture. Remove the meat and cut it into pieces.

Fry the mushrooms in half of the butter until the liquid is reduced, then add the rest of the butter and the flour and stir. Pour in the milk a little at a time and cook for 5 minutes. Add the lobster meat and most of the cheese—saving a bit to make the gratin. Season to taste with salt, pepper, and cognac. Fill the lobster shells with the mixture and top with the rest of the cheese.

Bake at 475°F (250°C) in the upper part of the oven until the cheese has melted and has gained a bit of color.

You can also mix store-bought Button mushrooms with dried wild mushrooms. It's not a bad idea to buy some fresh, store-bought mushrooms during the winter and mix your own frozen or dried mushrooms with it, as this gives you the taste and texture of fresh wild mushrooms.

If you wish to use Horse mushrooms, reduce the number used, as they have a very strong flavor. They also work well mixed with some mild-tasting Russula.

# FLAMMAN'S MILK CAP SALAD WITH SMOKED SALMON

*Flamman's Milk Cap salad with smoked salmon wrapped in flatbread makes for incredible picnic food. This salad also works well as part of a buffet.*

4 PORTIONS

- ¾ cup (150 g) blanched Rufous Milk Caps and/or Northern Milk Cap (see page 11)
- 1 tsp salt
- 1 red onion, finely chopped
- 1 tbsp mayonnaise
- 1⅓ cup (300 ml) yogurt
- 2 apples, finely chopped
- ½ cup pear, finely chopped
- ¾ inch (2 cm) celery, finely chopped
- salt and pepper

- 14 oz (400 g) smoked salmon or another smoked fish

Finely chop the Milk Caps and sprinkle a tsp of salt on top. Place them in a deep bowl with a weight on top. Place the chopped onion in cold water to dilute the taste.

Combine the mayonnaise and yogurt and add apples, pears, and celery.

Squeeze as much liquid as possible from the Milk Caps and mix into the salad. Drain the onion and add it to the salad, then season with salt and pepper.

Store the salad in a cool place for a few hours to allow the flavors to develop.

Serve with smoked fish and dark, whole-grain bread.

# LAMB STEW

*This stew is perfect when you are short on time or don't fancy standing at the stove for hours. The stew can be left to do its own thing and the longer you leave it, the better it will taste.*

4 PORTIONS

- 1–1½ quart (1–1½ liters) fresh mushrooms
- 2¼ lb (1 kg) lamb on the bone
- 3½ tbsp (50 ml) olive oil
- 1 can of peeled tomatoes, drained
- 4 garlic cloves
- 2 bay leaves
- 1 tsp dried rosemary
- 1 tsp dried thyme or 1 tbsp fresh
- 2 cups (500 ml) beef or mushroom stock
- 2 yellow onions, cut into wedges
- 3 carrots, sliced
- salt and pepper

Clean the mushrooms and cut into large chunks. Cut the meat into cubes and brown them in some of the oil in a frying pan. Then, remove them and transfer to a pot. Fry the mushrooms in the oil to brown them. Add them to the pot as well. Add salt and pepper, tomatoes, garlic, bay leaves, rosemary, and thyme and pour in enough stock to cover the meat. Cover and cook until the meat is tender, about 40 minutes.

Fry the onions and carrots in the rest of the oil and add them to the pot to cook through.

For this dish, you can use almost any mushroom, and it is nice to mix varieties. Why not use Trumpet Chanterelles? You can also swap some of the stock for red wine.

# VENISON STIR FRY

*A few years ago, a group of French mushroom pickers stayed with us. I made this dish with reindeer and lingonberries, and they thought the taste was deliciously exotic.*

4 PORTIONS

- 1 packet frozen, shredded venison (or reindeer, if available)
- 2 tbsp butter
- 1½ quarts (1½ liter) fresh mushrooms
- 2 yellow onions, chopped
- ¾ cup (200 ml) mushroom stock, made from a bouillon cube
- 10 juniper berries
- ½ tsp ground, dried rosemary, or 1 tsp fresh
- ½ cup (100 ml) cream
- ¼ cup (100 ml) cranberries (or lingonberries)
- salt and pepper

Brown the venison in half of the butter and transfer to a pot. Cut the mushrooms into smaller pieces and fry in the rest of the butter to brown them, then add the onion. Transfer to the pot and add the stock, juniper berries, and rosemary and cook uncovered for 10–15 minutes.

Add the cream and salt and pepper to taste. Finally add the cranberries or lingonberries.

Pelle often goes to Storlien in northern Sweden in the middle of August. While there, he picks Gypsy mushrooms, Orange Birch Boletes, Yellow Swamp Brittlegills, and *Russula paludosa*, which he dries and brings back home. This is the mushroom mix I use in my venison stir fry, but a lot of people have an abundance of Trumpet Chanterelles, and these work well, too.

You can also use lingonberry jam (available from IKEA, online, and specialty stores) if you can't find fresh or frozen lingonberries.

# PORK TENDERLOIN IN PUFF PASTRY

*I always serve my son-in-law pork tenderloin in puff pastry with Chanterelles as a birthday dinner, because it is his favorite dish. I'm not a huge fan myself, but what can you do!*

4 PORTIONS

- 1 lb (500 g) pork tenderloin
- butter for frying
- 7 oz s (200 g) frozen Chanterelles
- ½ cup (100 ml) crème fraîche
- cornstarch, optional
- 2 puff pastry sheets
- egg yolk
- salt and pepper

Clean the tenderloin and sear it in a pan with butter. Add salt and pepper. Wrap in foil and let cool.

Fry the Chanterelles in butter and add the crème fraîche. Make sure it is thoroughly combined and add some cornstarch if you so choose. Let cool.

Preheat the oven to 450°F (225°) and roll out the puff pastry into a rectangle that is a similar size to the pork loin. Place the meat on the dough and cover with the mushroom mixture. Press together the edges of the dough around the meat, making sure it is completely sealed, and brush with egg yolk. If you want to make it extra decorative, you can cut some leaves or other shapes out of any extra dough and place on top of the covered pork with the aid of a little water.

Bake for about 20 minutes. Use a meat thermometer to check that the meat is cooked through; the inner temperature needs to be 158°F (70°C). Serve with a salad.

You can also use beef tenderloin, which doesn't need to be cooked through—131°F (55°C) for rare, 140°F (60°C) for medium, and 158°F (70°C) for well done.

My son-in-law's favorite is the Chanterelle, but you can also use a mixture of mushrooms such as Trumpet Chanterelles, Yellow Foot, or Black Trumpets. Or you can even use store-bought Button mushrooms.

This is a great dish to serve guests, as you can prepare the meat and the sauce in advance. Just serve with a salad.

# LIGHTLY SALTED FILLET OF LAMB WITH WARM MUSHROOM SALAD AND THYME DRESSING

*Ten years ago we wrote the original edition of* Wild Mushroom Cookbook *in Swedish with chef Dieter Endom. This time, he has shared one of his best recipes with us to add some sparkle to the new edition.*

4 PORTIONS

*Salt marinade:*
- 2 cups (500 ml) water
- 2 tbsp salt
- 1 tsp granulated sugar
- 1 lb (500 g) lamb fillet
- Chinese soy sauce to glaze the meat
- 10½ oz (300 g) peeled potatoes, cut into wedges
- 10½ oz (300 g) fresh Slimy Spike Cap, Entire Russula, Arched Woodwax (*Hygrophorus camarophyllus*), and Gypsy mushroom, cut into pieces
- 1 tbsp olive oil
- 2½ cups (200 g) green beans, soaked
- 2 garlic cloves, chopped
- salt and coarsely ground pepper

*For the salad dressing:*
- 3 tbsp water
- 4 tbsp lemon juice
- 4 tbsp oil
- 1 tsp salt
- 1½ tbsp fresh, coarsely chopped thyme

Combine the ingredients for the marinade; the salt and sugar need to be completely dissolved. Place the lamb in the liquid for about an hour; it must be covered by the liquid.

Preheat the oven to 350°F (175°C). Remove the lamb from the marinade and let it drain; dry with paper towels. Brush the meat with the soy sauce and bake in the oven for 4–5 minutes on each side. Cook it slightly longer if you want it well done. Cover the meat in foil and let it rest.

Cook the potatos in lightly salted water until they are almost done, around 8–10 minutes. Drain and set aside.

Cook the mushrooms in a warm frying pan until all liquid is absorbed. Increase the heat, pour in the olive oil, and fry the mushrooms until they feel crunchy and start to pop in the pan. Add the potatos, beans, and garlic and fry for a few minutes until heated through. Season with black pepper.

Combine the ingredients for the dressing and pour on top of the mushroom salad.

# MUSHROOM LASAGNA

*Lasagna is a kitchen staple that tastes even better with mushrooms.*

**4 PORTIONS**

- 1 quart (1 liter) fresh mushrooms
- 5 tbsp olive oil
- 2 yellow onions, finely chopped
- 2 carrots, finely chopped
- 1½ oz (40 g) celeriac, finely chopped
- 9 oz (250 g) ground beef
- 1 can crushed tomatoes
- 1 tbsp concentrated meat or vegetable stock
- 4 tbsp red wine
- 1 cup (250 ml) water
- 1 tsp salt
- ½ tsp black pepper
- 9 oz (250 g) fresh lasagna noodles
- 1 cup (100 g) cheddar cheese, grated
- ½ cup (100 g) cream cheese
- ½ cup (100 ml) milk

Fry the mushrooms in a dry frying pan until all the liquid has been absorbed. Add some of the oil and fry the mushrooms until they start to brown, then set aside.

Fry the vegetables in the rest of the oil, add the ground beef, and brown the meat. Add crushed tomatoes, stock, red wine, and water and season with salt and pepper.

Place some of the ground beef at the bottom of a greased ovenproof dish and layer the lasagna, meat sauce, and mushrooms. Combine the cheese, cream cheese, and milk and pour over the top layer of lasagna. Place a few fried mushrooms on top and bake in the middle of the oven at 450°F (225°C) for 20 minutes.

# VENISON BURGERS WITH ORANGE BIRCH BOLETE AND PANKO-FRIED SHEEP POLYPORE

*For many years, Pelle has worked with Lena Flaten at a restaurant called Flamman, in Storlien, Northern Sweden. Mushrooms and wild plants feature heavily on the menu, and here is one of Lena's recipes—it's a real gourmet treat! When I first read the recipe, I made a mistake and thought it said* Russula decolorans, *which I didn't have at the time, so I used some mixed* Russula. *These worked well!*

4 PORTIONS

*Venison burger:*
- approx. 7 oz (200 g) fresh Orange Birch Bolete or another mushroom, preferably mixed mushrooms
- butter for frying
- 3 shallots, finely chopped
- 1 sprig fresh thyme or rosemary
- 3 crushed juniper berries
- approx. 12 oz (350 g) ground venison (or reindeer, if available)
- ⅔ cup (150 ml) cream
- salt and pepper

Finely chop the mushrooms. Fry in a pan without fat until the liquid is absorbed. Add butter and onion, and brown. Add chopped thyme, juniper berries, salt, and pepper and let cool.

Stir the cream into the ground venison and add the mushroom and onions. Add salt and pepper to taste.

Divide the meat in two chunks and create two thick rolls. Wrap first in plastic wrap and then in aluminum foil, making sure it is completely sealed. Place an ovenproof container of water in the oven, and place the rolls inside it. Preheat the oven to 275°F (130°C). Leave the rolls in the water bath until the core temperature of the meat reaches 131°F (55°C). Remove from the water and let rest.

*Lingonberry sauce:*
- 8 shallots, finely chopped
- 3 garlic cloves, finely chopped
- butter for frying
- 2 tbsp brown sugar

*(continued on page 105)*

- 3 sprigs rosemary
- ¾ cup (200 ml) red wine
- 1⅔ cup (400 ml) water
- 4 tbsp concentrated veal stock
- 1 tbsp balsamic vinegar
- light cornstarch, optional
- ¾ cup (200 ml) lingonberry jam (can be purchased at IKEA or online, or substitute cranberry jam)

Fry onion and garlic in butter until it starts to get some color. Add the sugar and stir until it has dissolved. Add rosemary, red wine, water, stock, and vinegar.

Boil until the liquid is reduced by half. Strain, and thicken with a bit of cornstarch if you so choose. Add the lingonberry jam and combine. Keep it warm or heat it up prior to serving.

*Cauliflower puree:*
- 1 small cauliflower
- 1 shallot, chopped
- 3½–7 tbsp (50–100 g) butter
- ¾ cup (200 ml) vegetable stock
- salt and pepper

Divide the cauliflower into florets. Fry the cauliflower and onion in some of the butter. Pour in the stock and boil until the cauliflower is soft. Drain. Puree the cauliflower with the butter. Add salt and pepper and keep warm.

*Panko-fried Sheep Polypore:*
- 4 Sheep Polypore caps
- ½ cup (100 ml) wheat flour or cornstarch
- 1–2 eggs
- 1¼ cup (300 ml) Panko breadcrumbs
- butter and oil
- salt and pepper

- approx. 2½ cups (400 g) broccoli florets

Cut the caps into equal-sized pieces. Dip the pieces first in flour, then in whisked egg, and finally in the Panko bread crumbs. Fry in butter and oil until golden brown and add salt and pepper. Keep warm. Boil the broccoli in salted water and keep warm.

Just before serving, divide each venison roll in two and cook on both sides on a griddle or grill pan.

Serve with the Sheep Polypore, cauliflower puree, broccoli, and a dash of lingon sauce. The rest of the sauce can be served alongside.

If you want to make a simpler meal, use ground beef. Divide into four burgers and fry in a pan. Boil the cauliflower and broccoli in stock; mix the cauliflower with a little butter and leave the broccoli whole. Use regular breadcrumbs for the Sheep Polypore and serve with lingonberry jam.

# OSSO BUCO WITH RUSSULA CAPS

*Russulas are gaining popularity among mushroom pickers, so why not use them to jazz up a classic Italian dish?*

4 PORTIONS

- ½ cup (100 ml) olive oil
- 14 oz (400 g) Russula caps
- 1¼ lb (600 g) veal shank, cut into slices
- 2 carrots, diced
- ⅓ cup (50 g) celeriac, diced
- 1–2 yellow onion, chopped
- 2 garlic cloves, chopped
- 14 oz (400 g) crushed or whole tomatoes
- 1 cup (200 ml) white wine
- 1 tsp salt
- ¼ tsp black pepper
- 1 bay leaf
- 2 tbsp veal stock (or 1 bouillon cube)
- 2 tsp dried thyme
- 2 tsp dried basil
- ½ lemon, zest

Heat some of the oil and brown the mushroom caps in batches. Set aside.

Brown the meat in a cast-iron pot in half of the remaining oil. Add the rest of the oil and the mushrooms and vegetables. Fry for a few minutes, then add tomato, wine, salt, pepper, bay leaf, and veal stock.

Cover and let simmer until the meat is tender, about 1–1½ hours. Add the herbs and half the lemon zest.

When ready to serve, sprinkle the rest of the lemon zest on top and some fresh herbs if you so choose. Serve with rice or pasta and a salad.

If you don't like veal, you can use ham hock (without the rind) or sliced lamb rack. Lamb takes about 45 minutes to cook through and pork about 1½ hours.

# ROAST BEEF WITH PORCINI AND GARLIC

*This is the best way to eat Porcini—fried in olive oil with garlic and parsley. This dish can be served with bread or, as in this case, with meat.*

4 PORTIONS

- 1 lb (500 g) roast beef or beef tenderloin cut into 4 pieces
- 1 quart (1 liter) fresh, sliced Porcini
- olive oil for frying
- 1–2 garlic cloves
- butter for frying
- chopped parsley
- salt and black pepper

Remove the meat from the fridge and let it warm to room temperature.

Fry the mushrooms in plenty of oil until brown, then reduce the heat and add the garlic—either chopped or pressed. Fry for a further 5–10 minutes over low heat. Add salt and pepper and sprinkle some parsley on top. Keep it warm.

Sear the roast beef or tenderloin for 2–3 minutes on each side, depending on how rare you like your meat. Season with salt and pepper.

Serve the meat with the Porcini mix, potato wedges, and a salad.

In Italy, Porcini is often prepared in this way. Try it with pasta and Parmesan, or on some fresh, white bread, preferably toasted.

# MUSHROOM PESTO

*Make this mushroom pesto when garlic mustard and nettles are in season.*

MAKES APPROX. 1½ CUP

- ½–¾ cups (100–200 ml) Wood Hedgehogs
- ¾ cup (200 ml) olive oil
- 1 quart (1 liter) nettles
- 10 leaves of garlic mustard
- 2 garlic cloves
- 1¾ oz (50 g) pine nuts or shelled almonds
- 3½ oz (100 g) grated Parmesan
- salt

Chop the mushrooms and fry slowly in a little of the oil until brown, then let cool.

Clean the nettles. Place them in boiling water and cook for 5 minutes.

Drain and rinse the nettles in cold water and squeeze out any excess liquid. Chop the nettles, and combine the mushrooms, nettles, garlic mustard, garlic, nuts, and Parmesan. Mix. Dilute with the olive oil and season with salt.

Nettles and garlic mustard can be picked when they have grown big, but only pluck the leaves at the top of the plants. St. George's mushroom and Sheep Polypore can also be used for this dish. Remember that the mushrooms must be cooked for at least 15 minutes before they can be used in the pesto.

Garlic mustard is a common weed that tastes slightly garlicky. You can also substitute the garlic mustard for ramson, which grows wild but can be bought in stores. If you have neither of these, you can just use more nettles.

# TOMATO SAUCE

*I often make this tomato sauce for barbecues, when I'll usually make a large batch. You can use any mushrooms you have, but I am partial to Scaly Tooth, which has a slightly smoky taste and a strong consistency. It can be sliced thinly without falling apart.*

6 PORTIONS

- 5 oz (150 g) fresh Scaly Tooth
- 2 yellow onions, finely chopped
- 2 garlic cloves, finely chopped
- 2 tbsp olive oil for frying
- 1 can crushed tomatoes
- 1 tbsp tomato puree
- 1 tsp sambal oelek or finely chopped red chili (optional)
- 2–3 tbsp ketchup
- basil, oregano, and thyme (fresh or dry)
- salt and pepper

Cut the mushrooms into strips and place in a saucepan with cold water. Bring to a boil and drain the water. Slowly fry the onion and garlic in half the olive oil over low heat until the onion turns translucent. Add the rest of the oil. Add the mushroom and fry for a few minutes, then add the crushed tomatoes, tomato puree, and, if you like, the sambal oelek. Increase the temperature and bring to a boil. Add ketchup and season to taste with salt and pepper. The sauce can simmer for a while. It needs to thicken; if it becomes too thick, you can add some water. Add chopped herbs and serve as a topping at a barbecue.

Sometimes I add a bouillon cube and a splash of red wine. If you're serving it with lamb, it can be nice to add some chopped mint to the sauce, and any leftovers can be served on pasta. If you have barbecue leftovers, you can dice them and toss into the sauce or you can fry some ground beef and add it to the sauce.

# MILK CAP SALAD

*The original Milk Cap salad was made from salted mushrooms. Variations on this salad are common in both Russia and Finland. You can read more about salting mushrooms on page 11.*

6–8 PORTIONS

- 3–3⅓ cups (700–800 ml) fresh Northern Milk Cap or Rufous Milk Cap
- 2 tsp salt
- 1 red or yellow onion, finely chopped
- 1 apple, finely chopped
- 1¼ cup (300 ml) crème fraîche or sour cream

Cut the mushrooms into smaller pieces and place in plenty of cold water. Bring to a boil and cook for 15 minutes. Rinse the mushrooms and drain, then toss with the salt.

Mix the onion and apple with the crème fraîche. Squeeze the liquid from the mushrooms, finely chop them, and add to the salad. Let cool for at least a few hours, but preferably overnight.

Serve on top of some dark bread and top it off with some caviar for a fancy starter, or serve it as a side dish at a buffet.

You can also serve it with herring or fermented Baltic herring.

I don't usually salt my Milk Caps; however, I tend to have a supply of precooked Milk Caps in the freezer that I use throughout the year to make Milk Cap salads and to pickle.

I usually don't measure too carefully when making this salad, but tend to gauge the amount needed depending on the number of Milk Caps I have. I usually take half as much onion and then the same amount of apple. Finally I add as much crème fraîche as I need to bind it. You can also use natural yoghurt or curd cheese, preferably mixed with crème fraîche or sour cream.

# BACON-WRAPPED MUSHROOMS

*This is a variation on bacon-wrapped dates that use mushrooms instead.*

MAKES 16

- 1 package of bacon
- 16 small, fresh mushrooms or mushroom pieces
- toothpicks
- oil for frying

Cut the bacon packet in half and roll up the mushroom pieces in a piece of bacon. Secure with toothpicks. Shallow fry in hot oil until they become crispy. Serve as an appetizer, either hot or cold.

Drain any remaining fat and pour into a glass jar. It can be used to fry mushrooms at a later date, as the bacon flavor goes well with mushrooms.

All firm mushrooms can be used for this dish: Boletales, Chanterelles, Sheep Polypore, Wood Hedgehog, or Scaly Hedgehog. Use small mushrooms or their stipes; large mushrooms should be cut into equal-sized pieces.

# STUFFED MUSHROOM CAPS

*Button mushrooms are great, as they look like small bowls when you remove the stipe. Small False Saffron Milk Caps and Russulas with a rolled-in margin can also be stuffed.*

24 PIECES

- 24 Button mushrooms
- 3½ tbsp (50 g) butter
- 2 garlic cloves, finely chopped
- 1 tsp breadcrumbs
- ¼ lemon, juice
- ¼ cup (50 ml) chopped parsley
- 1 tsp salt
- small pinch white pepper

Carefully remove the stipes by gently twisting them from the caps and place the caps on a greased, ovenproof dish. Finely chop the stipes and mix with the butter and other ingredients. Stuff the caps with this mixture.

Bake the mushrooms at 450°F (225°C) for roughly 20 minutes.

I often blend the stipes and garlic in a food processor. Then I'll add butter, breadcrumbs, and lemon juice and mix it all up. I add the chopped parsley last, because, if you run it through the food processer, the whole mixture will turn green!

You can also grill the stuffed mushroom caps if you like.

# DEEP-FRIED MUSHROOMS

*Deep-fried mushrooms are great when served with cocktails and taste best straight out of the deep fryer.*

- 1 quart (1 liter) small, fresh mushrooms, or 1 Wood Cauliflower cut into pieces
- 3¼ cups (750 ml) oil for frying
- salt

*Batter:*
- ¾ cup (200 ml) wheat flour
- 1 cup (150 ml) pilsner or pale lager
- 1 egg white

Clean the mushrooms; thin mushrooms, Trumpet Chanterelles, and Black Trumpets can be left whole if they are small. Cut the mushrooms into even-sized pieces. Combine the flour and beer and whisk until it is smooth. Whisk the egg white until stiff; make sure both the bowl and the whisk are clean before you begin. Fold the egg white into the batter.

Heat the oil to 350°F (180°C) in a saucepan with a thick bottom. The oil needs to be about 2 inches (5 cm) deep in the pan. Keep a lid handy lest the oil overheats; if it catches fire, covering it with the lid will help extinguish the flame (*never* pour water on it!). If you have a deep fryer, use that instead.

Dip the mushrooms into the batter and fry them a few at a time until they are golden brown. Turn them while frying to make sure they are evenly cooked. Place them on paper towels to drain and add salt. Serve as an accompaniment to cocktails.

# BACON-FRIED CHANTERELLES

*Fried Chanterelles on rye bread is an excellent reward for mushroom pickers after a long day of mushroom hunting!*

4 OPEN SANDWICHES

- 2 quarts (2 liters) fresh chanterelles
- 1 package of bacon, shredded
- 4 slices of hard rye bread
- salt and pepper

Place the Chanterelles in a frying pan. Leave them to cook in their own juices until the liquid is absorbed and the mushrooms are dry. Add the bacon bits and fry until the mushrooms have browned and the bacon is crispy. Season with salt and pepper.

Serve the bacon-fried Chanterelles on some tasty bread.

If you don't have 2 quarts (2 liters) of Chanterelles, you can mix in some Oyster mushrooms.

It's not just Chanterelles that taste great with bacon—Leccinum, small and firm Puffballs, and Trumpet Chanterelles are all delicious alternatives.

# PICKLED MUSHROOMS

*Pickled mushrooms work well with meat dishes—both ground as well as whole pieces.*

- 2 cups (500 ml) fresh, small mushrooms, any variety

*Brine:*
- ¼ cup (50 ml) vinegar
- ¼ cup (50 ml) olive oil
- ¼ cup (50 ml) water
- 1 tsp salt
- ¼ inch (1 cm) red chili, in thin rings
- 3 garlic cloves, divided lengthwise
- a few sprigs of fresh thyme, oregano, or basil; or a few lovage leaves

Small mushrooms can be left whole; larger ones should be cut in pieces.

Small Rufous Milk Caps look decorative when pickled, but they need to be blanched first; otherwise they'll taste too peppery. Place in plenty of cold water and bring to a boil. Cook for 10–15 minutes. Drain the water.

Combine the ingredients for the brine in a sauce pan and bring to a boil. Add the mushrooms and simmer for 10 minutes. Remove the herbs, as they will have wilted. Let cool. If you like, you can always add a fresh herb sprig.

The mushrooms can be served straight away but will taste even better if you let them sit in the fridge for 24 hours.

If you don't like chili, you can use red peppers instead. You can also use carrots and small onions; just double the brine, so it covers everything.

# JANNE SÄÄF'S PICKLED ST. GEORGE'S MUSHROOMS

- 1 lb (500 g) small, fresh St. George's mushrooms
- 1 tbsp salt

*Brine:*
- 1 cup (200 ml) white vinegar
- 1⅓ cups (300 ml) water
- ½ cup (100 ml) sugar
- ½ tsp mustard seeds
- 1 bay leaf
- 5 cloves
- 6 black peppercorns

*Herbs and vegetables:*
- 1 small carrot
- ¾ inch (2 cm) horseradish
- a few pieces of cauliflower
- salt
- ½ small green zucchini
- 1 pepper
- 1 whole red chili
- 1 garlic clove
- 2 blackcurrant leaves

Thoroughly clean and rinse the St. George's mushrooms and place in a saucepan. Add enough water to just cover the mushrooms. Add salt and boil for 10 minutes, then drain.

Combine the ingredients for the brine and boil in a pot, covered, for 15 minutes and let it set for at least an hour.

Rinse the vegetables and peel the carrot and horseradish. Slice the carrot. Boil the carrot and cauliflower in lightly salted water for a few minutes; they should retain a bit of crunch. Remove from the water and let them drain.

Chop the zucchini and pepper into chunks and thinly slice the horseradish. Make a few cuts in the chili so that it can soak up the brine. Layer the mushrooms and vegetables in a glass jar.

Bring the brine to a boil and pour into the jar. Cover immediately with a lid. Turn the jars upside down and store in a cool, dark place.

If you want a longer shelf life, after a few days you can place the jars in a pot and pour water into the pot, about ⅔ of the way up the jars. Slowly warm the water to 175°F (80°C) and wait 30 minutes. Then, allow the jars to cool in the water. If the lids seal properly, the mushrooms will keep this way for up to year.

# LEFTOVERS

Mushrooms are a great way to round out a dish. I often give leftovers a boost by adding some mushrooms.

Take a look in your fridge—is there anything that needs to be used right away? Don't get too hung up on the "best before" dates. Dairy products that have been stored in the fridge can be consumed as long as they still smell and taste fresh. This is true for eggs, too; eggs last a lot longer than their best-before dates.

If you have anything in the fridge with a "sell by" date, prepare it right away, as it will keep for another day when cooked or can be frozen. Sell-by dates are put on foods such as ground beef, fish, chicken, and so on.

Always smell the food; if food is kept too warm, it can go bad even before the sell-or best-before dates.

Sometimes you have scant leftovers, such as a piece of a chicken breast, or one or two spicy sausages or grilled steak. It might not be enough even for one person, but if you add some mushrooms and vegetables, you can create a whole new meal that can serve several people. In this chapter, we'll offer some suggestions on how to use food that might otherwise have been wasted.

*Cooked fish*

Do you have some leftover fish? Make the soup on page 27 and add some fish at the end. If you don't have any Weeping Milk Cap or Crab Brittlegills, use another mushroom, such as the Trumpet Chanterelle.

*Vegetables*

Are your carrots looking a bit sad? Do you have a dried piece of rutabaga or other root vegetables that have had their day? Remove any pieces that are turning bad and then peel and dice the part that's still good. Boil so they're almost soft and then drain, but keep the water. Chop an onion and slowly fry in some oil or butter until it is translucent. Fry the mushrooms to brown them and then add the vegetables until they soften. Add the onion, some salt and pepper, and sprinkle some herbs on top.

You can eat it as is or add a pressed garlic clove. If you have some sour cream or crème fraîche in the fridge, you can add this and some of the liquid you blanched the vegetables in and maybe even add a bouillon cube. Suddenly you have a sauce for pasta or meat.

### Eggs

Have you ever bought too many eggs and then worry that they are reaching their best-before date? I promise you will know if the egg is bad as soon as you crack it.

Make the oven-baked omelet on page 65. Crack each egg one by one into a cup and smell the egg before adding it to the others. That way you don't ruin the whole dish if one egg turns out to be bad.

### Soft bread

Bread that is starting to go stale can be cut into cubes and fried in butter, oil, or both to make croutons. Or you can mix melted butter with pressed garlic and spread it on a couple of slices of bread. Bake them at the top of the oven at 400–475°F (200–250°C) for 5–10 minutes. Both croutons and garlic bread taste great with soup (see page 23–35).

You can also make the mushroom sandwich with egg on page 67.

### Salad

Sometimes you make too much salad with your meal, and a day-old salad doesn't exactly taste great. However, if you turn it into stir fry, you can make a whole new dish out of it.

Iceberg lettuce, Chinese cabbage, and other cabbage or salad that is a bit wilted can also be fried in a wok. Remove any pieces that look brown or slimy before frying.

### Shredded Salad Stir Fry

- 1 quart (1 liter) fresh mushrooms, preferably with some Shiitake included
- oil, preferably with ½ tsp sesame oil
- 1 garlic clove, thinly sliced
- 1 onion, shredded
- ¼ inch (½ cm) red chili, finely chopped, or ½ tsp sambal oelek
- ¼ inch (½ cm) fresh ginger, finely chopped
- 1 carrot, shredded
- 1 leek, shredded
- salad, shredded

Fry the mushrooms in the oil until the liquid has been absorbed and the mushrooms start to brown. Add the garlic, onion, chili, and ginger and fry until the onion is soft. Add more oil if needed. Add the carrot, then the leek, and finally the salad. Serve as an accompaniment to another dish or add some cooked, shredded meat, and a bit of soy sauce. Serve with rice.

# CHICKEN LEFTOVERS

2 PORTIONS

- cooked chicken, equivalent to one chicken breast
- 2 yellow onions, in thin wedges
- 1 garlic clove, sliced
- canola oil for frying
- sambal oelek or fresh chili
- ¾ inch (2 cm) fresh ginger
- 1 quart (1 liter) fresh mushrooms or the equivalent amount of dried or frozen, preferably with some Shiitake included
- 2 carrots, in strips
- 1 savoy or white cabbage, shredded
- 2 tbsp Japanese soy sauce
- 5 oz (150 g) noodles
- salt and pepper
- ½ cup (100 ml) chicken stock + 2 eggs, optional

Shred the chicken finely. Gently fry the onion and garlic in a wok and add the sambal oelek and grated ginger.

If the mushrooms are fresh, steam them in a pan to remove the liquid. Then add them to the wok with the carrots and cabbage. Stir fry the vegetables until they start to soften but still have some crunch. Add the soy sauce.

Boil the noodles according the instructions on the packaging and add the cooked noodles and chicken to the wok. Season with salt and pepper.

If you want to add some more protein, mix the stock and egg and add it to the dish. Cook until the egg has set.

Dried Shiitake can be found in Asian groceries at a reasonable price and are great to have on hand in case you want to make a stir fry or another Asian-inspired dish. Remember to soak dried mushrooms before using (see page 13).

# LEFTOVERS FROM THE GRILL

4 PORTIONS

- 1 quart (1 liter) fresh mushrooms
- butter for frying
- 2 yellow onions, finely chopped, or an equivalent amount of pearl onions (for a fancier look)
- 2 garlic cloves, finely chopped
- 1 red pepper, diced
- 3–4 cups of leftover meat, diced
- ½ can crushed tomatoes or 1 tbsp tomato puree
- ½ cup (100 ml) red wine
- ½ cup (100 ml) beef stock
- parsley or other fresh herbs
- salt and pepper

Fry the mushrooms until the liquid is absorbed. Add the butter. Fry the mushrooms with the onion, pepper, and meat and add the tomato, wine, and meat stock. Cook for 5–10 minutes and season to taste with salt and pepper. Sprinkle with parsley and serve with blanched potatoes.

*Index*

Pork tenderloin in puff pastry  *97*
Root vegetable gratin with Gypsy mushroom  *49*

CHANTERELLE
Bacon-wrapped mushrooms  *119*
Bacon-fried Chanterelles  *125*
Mushroom egg sandwich  *67*
Mushroom pie with mozzarella and chard  *71*
Pork tenderloin in puff pastry  *97*
Yellow Foot, Chanterelle, and Leccinum pasta  *53*

CRAB BRITTLEGILL
Cod and white wine sauce with mushrooms  *85*
Fish soup, with or without fish  *27*
Mushroom burgers  *39*
Weeping Milk Cap blinis with dill  *55*

ENOKITAKE
Omelet with Enokitake and vegetables  *69*

ENTIRE RUSSULA
Lightly salted fillet of lamb with warm mushroom
    salad and thyme dressing  *99*
Lobster au gratin  *87*

FAIRY RING MUSHROOM
Cod and white wine sauce with mushrooms  *85*

FALSE SAFFRON MILK CAP
Stuffed mushroom caps  *121*
Maggan's False Saffron Milk Cap soup  *33*
Mushroom egg sandwich  *67*
Tina's best Trumpet Chanterelle soup  *31*

GYPSY MUSHROOM
Lightly salted fillet of lamb with warm mushroom
    salad and thyme dressing  *99*
Root vegetable gratin with Gypsy mushroom  *49*
Venison stir fry  *95*

HORSE MUSHROOM
Lobster au gratin  *87*

LECCINUM
Bacon-fried chanterelles  *125*
Weeping Milk Cap blinis with dill  *55*
Yellow Foot, Chanterelle, and Leccinum pasta  *53*

MATSUTAKE
Bredberg's soup  *35*

MIXED MUSHROOMS
Vegetable pie with mushrooms  *73*
Pelle's mushroom soup  *25*
Pork tenderloin in puff pastry  *97*
Quinoa and mushroom salad  *47*
Root vegetable gratin with Gypsy mushroom  *49*
Mushroom egg sandwich  *67*
Mushroom pie with mozzarella and chard  *71*
Tina's best Trumpet Chanterelle soup  *31*

NORTHERN MILK CAP
Flamman's Milk Cap salad with smoked salmon  *89*
Milk Cap salad  *117*

ORANGE BIRCH BOLETE
Venison burgers with Orange Birch Bolete and
    panko-fried Sheep Polypore  *103*
Venison stir fry  *95*

**OYSTER MUSHROOM**
Bacon-fried chanterelles *125*
Mushroom dumplings *51*

**PARASOL MUSHROOM**
Breaded Parasol mushrooms *43*

**PORCINI**
Porcini foccacia *61*
Porcini carbonara *45*
Roast beef with Porcini and garlic *109*
Mushroom egg sandwich *67*

**PUFFBALL**
Bacon-fried Chanterelles *125*

**RUFOUS MILK CAP**
Flamman's Milk Cap salad with smoked salmon *89*
Milk Cap salad *117*

*RUSSULA PALUDOSA*
Venison stir fry *95*

**SCALY HEDGEHOG**
Bacon-wrapped mushrooms *119*

**SCALY TOOTH**
Tomato sauce *115*

**SHEEP POLYPORE**
Bacon-wrapped mushrooms *119*
Venison burgers with Orange Birch Bolete and
　Panko-fried Sheep Polypore *103*
Mushroom hash *57*

**SHIITAKE**
Bredberg's soup *35*
Chicken with Black Morel *81*

Chicken leftovers *133*
Mushroom dumplings *51*
Shredded salad stir fry *131*

**SLIMY SPIKE CAP**
Lightly salted fillet of lamb with warm mushroom
　salad and thyme dressing *99*

**ST. GEORGE'S MUSHROOM**
Janne Sääf's pickled St. George's mushrooms *129*
St. George's mushroom soup with nettles and ground
　elder *23*

**TRUMPET CHANTERELLE**
Bacon-fried chanterelles *125*
Chicken with Black Morel *81*
Lamb stew *93*
Omelet with Enokitake and vegetables *69*
Root vegetable gratin with Gypsy mushroom *49*
Pork tenderloin in puff pastry *97*
Mushroom egg sandwich *67*
Mushroom pie with mozzarella and chard *71*
Tina's best Trumpet Chanterelle soup *31*
Cod and white wine sauce with mushrooms *85*
Trumpet Chanterelle soup with gorgonzola *29*
Venison stir fry *95*

**VELVET BOLETE**
Mushroom egg sandwich *67*

**WEEPING MILK CAP**
Weeping Milk Cap blinis with dill *55*
Fish soup, with or without fish *27*
Mushroom burgers *39*
Cod and white wine sauce with mushrooms *85*

*When we are out and about giving lectures on edible mushrooms and how to use them, we are frequently asked which are our favorites! Of course, we both have favorites, and often from the same species but not always in the same order. So here they are, in no particular order: Crab Brittlegill,* Lactarius volemus, *Parasol Mushroom, Porcini, and Black Trumpet. These mushrooms differ so immensely when it comes to taste that it is impossible to pick one over the other. Our preferences depend a lot on how mushrooms are prepared and what food and drink is served as an accompaniment.*

CONVERSION CHART
*We have created a chart to roughly show how much precooked and dried mushrooms you get from fresh mushrooms. In this way, we hope it will be easier for you to convert the recipes according to which mushroom you plan to use. 1 quart (1 liter) fresh mushroom gives you 1¼ cups (300 ml) cups precooked or ½– 1¼ cups (100–300 ml) dried mushrooms. Mushrooms that have been cooked and then frozen are calculated the same way as precooked mushrooms in this table.*

| FRESH MUSHROOMS | PRECOOKED MUSHROOMS | DRIED MUSHROOMS | MUSHROOM FLOUR |
|---|---|---|---|
| 1 quart (1 liter)........... | 1¼ cups (300 ml)........... | ½–1¼ cups (100–300 ml)...... | ½ cup (100 ml) |
| 7–10½ oz (200–300 g).... | 7–10½ oz (200–300 g)...... | ¾–1 oz (20–30 g).............. | ¾–1 oz (20–30 g) |